A Heart's Betrayal Workbook

A Heart's Betrayal Workbook

Tools for Women and Men
Recovering from Divorce
and Broken Relationships

A BIBLE STUDY

Christine Cantilena Barnes, LPC

Copyright © 2024 by Christine Cantilena Barnes

All rights reserved. No part of this book may be reproduced or transmitted in any form or by any means, electronic or mechanical, including photocopying, recording, or any information storage and retrieval system, without permission in writing from the author.

ISBN: 978-1-6653-0937-0

This ISBN is the property of BookLogix for the express purpose of sales and distribution of this title. The content of this book is the property of the copyright holder only. BookLogix does not hold any ownership of the content of this book and is not liable in any way for the materials contained within. The views and opinions expressed in this book are the property of the Author/Copyright holder, and do not necessarily reflect those of BookLogix.

∞This paper meets the requirements of ANSI/NISO Z39.48-1992 (Permanence of Paper)

0 9 1 1 2 4

changinghopecounseling.com

To my amazing friends and family who were such a support and motivation for the completion of my books. Each chapter has great meaning to me and reveals various seasons in my life, both of joy and great pain. As I am finally able to look down from the hill of victory, I can see how life's significant pain has led to the growth inside me. This has made me the strongest version of myself. My guardian angel never left my side nor did God the Almighty. I hope my experiences will lead you in the direction of attaining the authentic meaning of true love and healthier relationships.

Here's to the boy who thought I hung the moon and gave me great purpose! My sweet son Romeo. I cherish you more than you will ever realize with so many powerful memories that we have made together. Your brightness shines in my heart always. May you have eternal integrity, honor, and character always. I pray that you learn from my mistakes and always keep God in the center of your relationships. My prayer is simple; for people to continue to say and believe, "Your son has the heart of a godly servant."

Always know where your TRUE NORTH LIES. Betrayal is the ultimate sacrifice of one person for a heart's desire at any cost, even including our wedding vows. Understanding your true north, value, and moral system can help a person fight against the most relentless tidal wave of grief, shame, and recovery.

Contents

Introduction		*ix*
Thoughts		*xi*
Chapter 1	Who Are You and What Are You Made Of?	1
Chapter 2	Commitment and What Does It Really Mean About Me?	15
Chapter 3	How Do Others Harm Us: Domestication, Censorship, Co-Dependency, and Narcissism	33
Chapter 4	How Do We Escape Dysfunctional Relationships and Health Issues?	45
Chapter 5	Effects on Our Children (Depression, Anxiety, PTSD) from Divorce and Broken Relationships?	59
Chapter 6	Legal Considerations and Extra Knowledge	71
Chapter 7	Mental Prison and Mental Health	85
Chapter 8	Reconciling and Forgiving: A Healing Homecoming	97
Chapter 9	Singleness and Rediscovering Yourself	107
Resources		*119*

Introduction

You may be asking yourself why your marriage or relationship has taken this unexpected turn in life. How you will be strong enough to rebuild your life during and after the process of the divorced relationship. I realize that I have lived in a fictitious marriage for many years, losing myself in the process, and now I am realizing it is time to get back to who I am.

Any relational breakup is a life-changing event. The following pages come from a heartfelt sense of transparency. I chose my rock-solid following of God for my support and counsel. That is not to say the suffering was not intense and horrific. I was able to move forward and still have purpose in my life. Joy can be restored.

> "So, with you: Now is your time of grief, but I will see you again and you will rejoice, and no one will take away your joy." John 16:22 NIV

Joy and peace can all be achieved with great effort and continued belief in yourself and who you were created to be. One of the most important endeavors you are to face is knowing who you are now and who you will become after such a personal tragedy. It is like being in a deep well and sinking to the very bottom until one day you realize that you are better than that.

Many confusing thoughts will arise out of the ashes of your marriage or broken relationship. Will everyone still embrace you the same after your divorce? How does divorce change our inner souls and outlooks on life? What will it feel like to not be married any longer? Will non-divorced people ever understand the depths of defeat and damage that many divorces leave behind, and still have empathy for you?

The answers are all in the pages to follow. My downward journey of divorce began one hot summer day when my young son and I were riding in the car with my former husband. We were catching a plane to Florida for a summer vacation. I knew for many months that our status quo in the marriage was off kilter (less time together, more work involvement, more distance intimately). I chose not to look at the status of our marriage for fear of knowing my great intuitions and suspicions were true. I will tell you to always listen to your intuition and your gut. It is generally right.

My story all began when I truly and whole-heartedly experienced the meaning of bittersweet. It happened in slow motion, such as being in a movie, while each painful moment took my breath away leaving me in utter sadness and confusion. I am not sure which had the biggest impact over my future. First it was the supposition of divorce, then the loss of my best friend of 40 years, later, the loss of seeing my only son (alienation at its best), and during all that trauma, being forced to move from my family home and establish a financially stable career in my mid-fifties. Only God could have kept me alive in late night moments of despair.

Prior to these events, life was anything but normal at home, however one thing was constant, the love of my only son. It seemed like water rushing through my fingers as my life was changing quicker than I could process. It is still hard to go back to the relentless truth that unfolded in 2015 and continued to rage shock waves in my life for many years following.

Thoughts

Sadness is interesting. The word almost sounds tame. Divorce and separation are anything but just sadness. They are daunting events that take place in life and wreak havoc over one's life for many years after. Divorce is similar to the energy and devastation that make mountains crumble. I believe the forest weeps at night for those who suffer, dissipating by one's divorce. As soon as the word "divorce" is out in the universe it cannot be taken back. It begins to encrypt mayhem a bit at a time. Like a once beautiful flower slowly rotting. It takes the utter stink to make some people realize that their relationship has already died right in front of their nose. By the time your brain catches up the damage is done.

It is hard to conceptualize that your childhood best friend, husband, and children could vanish in your life. Be taken, not without a fight, but nevertheless gone from your known existence. Unfortunately, this happens a hundred times a day or more in our world. It is time to suit up and become a warrior. Ask God for courage and great strength and for what you are about to encounter. There will be days when you are grateful that you got out of the battle alive but still feel slain. It is the hardest mental workout you may ever endure. Do not let your thoughts hold you hostage. Instead, surround your wisest counsel and faithful friends to support you during the process. Move back home if you need. Take the pressure off to think clearly. Find a good therapist who is sympathetic and well-educated in grief and divorce. Make sure they have walked the path.

Your children's suffering from divorce is heart breaking. You can buffer some of the pain and they may reside in therapy before it is over. They may turn on you through alienation and you still have God to protect you. Prayer is your best option. It will hold your sanity together and give you peace during the malicious battle that is now unleashed on you and your family. Take refuge is a good support system.

Christians you need to take heed and remember what times we are living in today. Paul talked about these times of wickedness to come in II Timothy Chapter 3. It is very daunting, but we must have our eyes opened to reality. There will be a time when men will call right to be wrong, and wrong to be right, and we will see more divorce upon our nation as individuals and as a community. These are some truthful Bible verses which you can rely as truth. There will be Godlessness in the Last Days. I can only imagine the amount of pain, suffering, and difficulty that is still to come. The Bible is clear that people will be lovers of self, money, and it will be obvious in the appearance of their proudness, abusiveness, arrogance, and overall disobedience. It makes me so sad to know that children will turn on their parents who gave them life and the ungratefulness and unholy will be left behind. If this truth does not give you chills, know that this is just the tip of the iceberg. People will become even more heartless than we know now. The lack of self-control will be brutal, and people will rise the height of slander and recklessness beyond what we can fathom.

After reading these words, it makes you think how humankind even made it thus far. There is so much sin and selfishness in this world and it will get worse at the end of times. God gives us tools to defeat many situations causing pain and suffering in our current world. We need to protect our minds, hearts, bodies, and who we keep close to us more than ever.

Find joy and compassion in the love for nature and pets.

Chapter One

Who Are You and What Are You Made Of?

I believe the consciousness of our soul mixed with our faith governs who we are and want to be. This part of body connects to our brain and is often tussling in a spiritual battle from time to time. The assimilation of good and evil seem too often rule our behaviors and decision-making process. I am partial to believing that integrity and positive character are present in everyone and therefore, we are capable of being great people together in society. This may beg the question if are we born with goodness or sinfulness? At the beginning of grad school, I remember being asked a poignant question on an exam. Are we born good or sinful? I want to believe we are born good, and the world takes hold of us, molds us, and we become a mix or good and less perfect attributes. I understand that the Bible teaches that we are born sinners and I do agree. As we age, we begin to learn our shortcomings and our natural talents and strengths, only then do we authentically know ourselves. We are such complex creatures on a pendulum changing at all stages of life. With God we do have the ability to be humble and kind through life even when faced with rigorous experiences.

Now if we introduce separation in a relationship or divorce to our nurturing environment, then what happens? Is the act of separation and divorce inherently good or bad? Maybe it is both? Remember that the Bible and Ten Commandments are our source of guidance for a better path in life. God gives us information on divorce as well as how to avoid it, as the Ten Commandments reference "Do not covet your neighbor." Unfortunately, we can only control our own behavior and not the behavior of those we marry. A great loss of hopes and dreams are instantly solen away from us and mental suffering begins as soon as our vows are broken. Divorce is described from many to be as one of the most painful events to experience in life. This leads us to wonder if the process and aftermath of divorce will have the power to change our natural goodness and spiritual direction?

All these questions will be answered in this book.

Let's assume that we are meant to find our one and only love on this earth. When we do, it seems like our journey of singleness is over forever. We have great hope and joy to have a family one day and stay happily married. Unfortunately, there are too many causes that steal that dream all too often. We can be from the best upbringing and still trust someone who promises to stay with us to our last dying day, and then chose not to honor this commitment. We can try to pinpoint why this happens so often and many answers lie in our level of truth within ourselves to stay committed to one person for "better or worse forever."

Who we are is seen through many different lenses. On the website, Verywellmind.com, February 2024, the writers Kate Nelson and Nick Ingalls [1] state that personality is a major part of what defines us as human beings. It is believed that personality combines our emotional, behavioral, and intellectual components of how we choose to interact in this world. They go on to explain that while there may be undeviating parts of our personalities, they generally progress as a combined result of our environments. Experiences continue to shape us and have the power to influence our future personas.

This leads me to hypothesis that as trials and tribulations begin affecting us so does the erosion of marriage vows and betrayal. When times are tough, our true self emerges as either an amazing person of victory or a weak-minded victimized individual. Sometimes the stress leads our decision-making ability to be shocking to ourselves and others. Many of us are co-dependent in life. The need of another person is so great we lose who we are. We wear masks and become unsteady and unsure of our true self. It takes sometimes takes a tragedy to see what we are made of underneath. We either rise to the occasion or not because two people with contrite hearts cannot make it through a long-term commitment no matter who they are.

I still grapple with my thoughts about relationships and the fulfillment it can provide us. We cannot meet all our needs through a relationship. Being grounded in ourselves and have the excitement of sharing a life with another is important. Sometimes after years of dating or marriage we will require reconnecting with old friendships. This can be a problem for friendless couples due to the neediness and unhealthy co-dependence on one another. Loneliness was never od's plan.

Historically, many marriages have less than a fair chance of sustaining long-term commitment. This is nothing new and can be seen through past generations. However, I believe that this thought can change by closer examination of yourself. Positive changes can alter our viewpoint and inner perspective. I always say to my clients, "Turn the dial to the next channel for a better outlook." We are creatures of habit and tend to not like change and would rather 'go with the flow'. For success in marriages, we must concede and compromise on many things to allow both people a fighting chance of happiness. There is distorted thinking from some that feel like they get one shot at marriage and cannot imagine doing life alone. This is not a healthy or holistic view in coupling. This is somewhat of a love addiction issue which does not equal commit in a relationship.

God announces in chapter one of the Bible (Genesis) that we are creatures that need a partner, helpmate, and made the union of husband and wife. God knew right away about us there was no secret that mankind is happier when in pairs. There is nothing easy about putting two completely different humans together and thinking of everlasting bliss. The sanction of marriage may be one of the hardest things in this life to master. When I was married, I rarely thought of our different economic status, parental teachings, and faith divergence. I thought a Christian was indeed a Christian and true love was just that. These two things equaling a fine marriage for life was a distortion.

Through my 22 years walking in my former marriage, I have learned there are some many Christian beliefs under the huge umbrella named Christianity. These beliefs can become major or minor elements that can help us to become more united or more divided which separates us. I never dreamed that love would fail me, or my faith could become one of the reasons to leave a marriage. Even so, I understand that I am stronger for this decision and to be true to the boundaries surrounding what I believe. God does not expect a person to stay in a marriage that causes harm. This is hard for anyone to endure and even harder to accept the loss of what was a marriage. That being said, God still hates divorce.

From the beginning of conception God was working out the details of our individual personality and how much the body and mind could endure. Our mental and physical pain is like a bucket of water. This bucket can fill to the top but should not run over. When that happens, we are not functioning as God designed us. God made certain to put into place inner strengths to deal with many hardships. Did you know that your childhood experiences can have vast strongholds on your future relationships? If we watch our parents suffer through their marriage, then we have a new cognition of what the holiness of marriage looks like. The more trauma we endure and are subjected too, it is possible we lose a bit of our innocence towards holy matrimony.

We can think we really know ourselves but until you feel at peace with what you have become and your sole purpose in life, you do not really know your entire self. Some people are more in tune with the sturdiness of who they are while others view themselves as fragile and unsure. Truth is we are discovering bits and pieces of ourselves throughout life. Knowing your weaknesses or blind spots is imperative. Some of these experiences are life changing and monumental for growth. Other times, shocking, anxiety invoking, and negligent.

The later can linger on for years. Unfinished business is what psychology calls issues from the past that the present cannot reconcile. Peace is not easily attained in this state. The future of a person is dependent on reconciliation for past hurts. As a therapist, I recommend closure of the past as it is key to having a healthy future of self and in marriages.

There are many techniques to get to know yourself better and improve your future interpersonal interactions. Quizzes are one method to score yourself on many different levels. Some being, humble, loving, introverted, extroverted, successful, and so much more. Through time and experiences our temperament may change, hence, we change. We need to be aware if we are living the life that God meant for us by knowing ourselves inside out. The fruits of the spirit are real and can always be mastered and improve our stance on life. We do not always get it right, and plenty of choices are in front of us.

Chapter One Exercises

Small group format: 45 minutes

Knowing yourself well is a large part of preparing yourself for many hardships in life.

1. Are you a product of nature or nurture? Explain?

2. Do you feel that you are being tested in your spiritual journey? Do you have the strength and support to continue down the road of uncertainty?

3. How are you handling your suffering? Do you use healthy coping skills? What are they?

4. Why do you think we endure difficult situations and trauma? What trauma have you witnessed? Has it changed you? For the better or worse?

5. What are your unhealthy coping skills?

6. Do you need more healthy coping skills? List 5 of them.

7. Our strengths can be like superpowers if we are able to tap into them and move in a positive direction, knowing our strength and what we are capable of after enduring through hard times.

8. What are you best strengths? Look at the quiz results.

9. Is your bucket overflowing? What are your weaknesses? How can you avoid the pitfalls?

10. Do you compliment yourself on your strengths and have self-compassion?

11. Do you have a daily affirmation? Favorite verse? Mantra?

12. How often do you work on improving your weaknesses? How much time is really needed? How can you add this to your daily schedule?

13. If you are spiritual, do you look at your faith as the center for strength and courage?

14. Is suffering something that has replayed since childhood? Are you angry at God? Can suffering help you? How?

15. Your blind spots in life can sneak up and be partially responsible for poor decisions that are being made again and again. Would you like to ask for help?

16. How can you minimize your blind spots?

17. How well do you know your spouse, partner, or person you are dating?

18. Are you co-dependent on a relationship? Why is this unhealthy?

19. What fruits of the spirit are you practicing and mastering?

Begin taking a few quizzes to get to know yourself and others better: Know who is out to destroy you and your family.

https://www.linkedin.com/pulse/pondering-career-change-online-assessments-might-help-brooks/

https://pathofselflove.org/assessments/self-love-quiz/

https://psycho-tests.com/test/lusher-color

https://www.temperamentquiz.com/

https://happierhuman.com

Chapter Two

Commitment and What Does It Really Mean About Me?

Let us begin with what you know. Is it based on what you can see, touch, and hear? Have you graduated to a more spiritual belief of the unseen in regard to commitment? A great Bible verse to remember is knowing Christ even without sight or vision. This concept seems odd, and yet, we make commitments to Christ as believers. Even when we do not know the future. We do not give up on our creator, we stand tall in our commitments that we make before God, such as a wholesome marriage… remember for better or worse, sickness or health?

What was your exact vows that you said? Can you even remember? Did you ever have those commitments anywhere in your home as a reminder and encourager? Before you entered the destruction zone in your relationship were you still open enough to hear God's voice? Did you pray for unity and continued nourishment before your engagement or marriage? I personally did pray for God's blessing but did not wait to clearly hear the answer. I think that I wanted to hear it so bad that my feelings took over and I heard what I wanted to as a newly engaged woman.

I did not pray with my family about the wedding nor did our families together pray for it. I will do things differently next time now that I have better insight to share with others. Make sure that you and your family feel God's blessing upon you, and it has an everlasting bearing on your marriage. Make sure to never stop praying for your commitment to be protected and nourished by God. When God truly brings us together then we stay together through constant awareness of who and what we surround ourselves and lives with. Some of us are taught commitment from a very young age and embrace it deeply. Our parents and mentors play a very important part in this matter and enhance our ability to carry out true commitment. We are either in the camp of honoring commitment or not. We tend to live our life according to our values, beliefs, and environment. Commitment is like an onion with many layers to it and certainly can bring may tears if not safeguarded.

It pains me to explain that from personal experience the fact of knowing right from wrong is not a guarantee that years of living with someone will make a marriage of pure devotion. Being married has no guarantee that your partner will continue to grow in integrity and their loyalty with you. Commitment is nothing short of truly understanding your true north, Godly strengths, and divine inner strength to uphold your values and morals. In life there not many other things trump the act of commitment. It shows what you are made of, self-control, and your perseverance above all to follow Christ. Long-term commitment is only possible with the support of family, worthy friends, immense inner character, high morals, unreproachable ethics, and a constant re-grounding in faith. Tough times will come and go in relationships, and the well balanced and healthy ones will survive.

The Gottman's have been in the business of keeping marriages healthy and whole. They have a positive relationship teaching called the 4 Horseman. It simply states that if you are willing to break one of the 4 Horseman rules then the consequences will not be good for the relationship. The Gottman's believe that good and positive communication is the key. Here are the rules that I practice when helping clients stay together in therapy. Remove Criticism, Contempt, Defensiveness, and Stonewalling from fighting. Instead love each other enough to stay engaged, take breaks when needed, be respectful, and remember this person that you married is supposed to be your best friend.

There are many reasons that some may not be able to keep fair fighting rules and lose their commitment little by little until it has vanished. Physical and emotional abuse are high on the list. Afterall, who wants to be a doormat? Second, the desire to be single again, and third, the lack of desiring to make things work through difficult times. Without great control, prayer, and guidance, abuse is not tolerable long-term. It is heartbreaking that someone you vowed your entire life could hurt you in the worst ways. This lack of commitment and respect are so destructive to your soul that it generally requires departing the relationship. This forced act of ending your commitment is essential to your well-being. Many people love so deep they are willing to leave their commitment under great and continual abusive circumstances. Physical and emotional abuse are not healthy, and one cannot survive long in a one-sided relationship. Your mind and body begin to break down without consistent love and support. The tearing down of our minds is horrifying. To try to understand the depths of someone who chose you to condemn, shame, and betray is wicked. I cannot think of a more fitting word, except living in a realm of grief.

Another common type of committal break is when you are forced to end your marriage because your partner is determined to single again or enjoys a less monogamous relationship by playing the field. This is like being high on endorphins all day long. This is self-serving and can lead to dual relationships, which most never signed up for. It is not uncommon to be served with divorce papers after the high wear off and they realize their life is boring and they deserve more. The adulteress spouse is willing to put your dreams and hopes at risk of fruition, so that they instead can be happy. This breed of person can have such a lack of self-esteem and commitment that they are willing to put someone above you. Worse is their lack of self-control that they decide to have an affair. This seems to put excitement in their life over their faith, family, and prior commitments. God reminds us again and again in the Bible without self-control we are opening ourselves to great vulnerability for enemy attacks and wanting to savor ungodly passions. God has so many warnings on this topic. This is one of my favorites verses that I used in prayer for my marriage.

Humans Lack Self-Control… That's Why We Need God!
"Do not deprive each other except perhaps by mutual consent and for a time, so that you may devote yourselves to prayer. Then come together again so that Satan will not tempt you because of your lack of self-control." 1 Corinthians 7:5 NIV

When I was married, I could see signs of a lack of self-control financially in myself. I also saw things that broke my heart with my spouse. My financial shortcomings could never hold a candle to what I endured over the years. My strong honor to never break a marriage vow was something that I was taught as a child. I never wavered once, not even at the final day of the divorce. Not once did I have thoughts about kissing another man, being held tightly by someone else, or anything that even looked as much as an inappropriate advance.

Even as lonely as I was in my marriage, I will never understand how a married person could be so willing to put their marriage at risk for their own excitement. The amount of energy that some spouses put into serving their own feelings and emotions through instant gratification is painful to watch and endure. It never becomes easier to see their level of self-centeredness, pride, and lack of pure devotion for their spouse. You may even witness levels of volatile anger when you try to challenge them. High levels of risk taking can be seen by others as well. Without truly divine friendships and accountability, you may feel alone and unsupported.

At the end of my 22 years of marriage a stranger came to deliver the news. This person who served me my divorce papers. She stood cold in the moment with lifeless eyes and threw the divorce papers as I was lowering my car window in my driveway. My hopes and dreams were snuffed out in seconds. It was the weekend of Mother's Day. I was so hurt that I cried in my car until my son arrived from school. My son and I knew it was coming because my former husband had taken him aside one afternoon at home and told him without my knowledge. My son was the first to hear of the divorce from that incident. He called me seconds later while I was shopping for dinner in the grocery store.

I remember losing all my thoughts as I raced home to intervene with the atrocious behavior of telling a child about the divorce without my presence. His father had shown him on the computer the Georgia law, about what children can do when reaching the age of thirteen. My son learned that could have my rights as a mother and caregiver terminated, leave our home, and instead live with his father. He was only age twelve at the time and surely did not need this burden on him to have to decide. This was like a wildfire spreading in me, and this knowledge put into motion the poisonous consequences that began for the next six years to come.

After being served the divorce papers, getting out of the car, when I walked into the house, I remember that my head spinning, and my feet were no longer planted firmly on the ground. I felt like I had been punched in the stomach again and again. My life as I knew it would be changed forever now. My mind instantly fast forwards to Thanksgiving and Christmas. My visions of the future seemed to be a very sad situation that I do not want to validate. No longer will it be a holiday celebrated as family. It will be a gambit of coerced holidays fighting to see which of us will have our son beside us. I often wondered as many do, how God allows this heartbreak. I decided he is bigger than me and all experiences have a purpose. It is not worth getting stuck in this thought.

While my family did talk of divorce, my parents stayed together. It was a promised made and honored. It was not a perfect marriage as none are, but still a role model to follow through thick and thin. I believe a more positive thought is the action of working on how to keep your moral compass. In my readings I believe there are four main avenues to do this. In my graduate program I learned about psychologist Lawrence Kohlberg who studied and wrote about moral development. His insight was amazing and open our minds to how different morality can set apart in boy's verses girls and in various cultures. This is seen from birth when a child is raised to have purpose and success in life is done by following a moral direction of not hurting others. This practice has many facets and mainly we can observe the following. First, there are absolute and relative beliefs. The absolute is the unchanging and universal ones. For example, do not kill, do not steal, and respect property. Then the relative principles are basically what is believes by most depending on the circumstances. For instance, an underage teen kills their parents. In court, there is mitigating circumstances that play a part in the overall belief of punishment. There is an understand of a clear right from wrong in life which may also have to be analyzed with extra data of the mental capacity when the act when done. Second, adhering to your moral principle that you have given your word. This can be different for some due to alcohol, drugs, and influences of others that alter our beliefs. Third, the impact of moral principle. This can affect who you are and how you want others to identify you. For instance, if you are a Christian, not all will accept you and you may have to defend your honor. If this task is too difficult, then your morality can shift or decreasing causing horrific consequences, hence losing your marriage and loving family. Adultery seems to be a big moral question for some. Our society is ever changing and does not always ethically hold the belief that adultery is a detriment to a marriage. I say, they have not lived that journey or deeply embraced their faith.

When it does come to ending your marriage, the puzzle of the proper exiting is very complex, and you will need a plan. I am here today to help you unwind some difficult thoughts you may have on divorce. If you are anything like me, you may have only had good thoughts about marriage and children. Divorce could have possibly been the most shocking work you ever had to face. I think it is a word that Satan dreamed up to destroy women and families. Shattering true and divine love of commitment. Divorce makes us react and respond to stimuli we are not accustomed to. It is possible to rise above the pain of divorce but not without subsequent scars.

You may still feel defeated in the moment but can have a healthy parting instead of a vindictive one. Endurance and resilience will get you through at a steady haul. Gaining insight into how to survive a broken commitment will enhance your ability to heal and recover successfully. Some of my advice may seem like common sense to some but difficult and confusing for others. This is why healthy insight from others can be valuable and prideful advice can be dangerous.

Faith has guided me through my only marital relationship, with God lifting the insurmountable pain from me. I probably know myself better than ever now, and have maintained my commitment to Christ, never once wavering during the trauma of my divorce. I understand forgiveness and the supernatural power of God more intensely during the time after divorce. I am here to tell you there is light at the end of the divorce tunnel. God gives us beautiful things and can take them away at any moment. This does not have to be perceived as negative. God knows us better than anyone on this earth. Never forget that He is our Father. He opens so many doors for us. Certain situations must perish for goodness to be seen again and a door to open.

The key to emerging with a new, hopeful vantage point is to arise from the depths of a divorce and its battlefield instead of staying in it. We can regain acceptance of our true value once we escape the memories of our damaged selves, which divorce can replay constantly to us. Just for a moment, believe in commitment again. With great determination, you will start learning to see truth about yourself again as you believe in commitment.

Does personal willpower of commitment overshadow who we really are including our willpower? If we are weak-minded, then we will certainly lack the willpower in sustaining great commitment. Without true commitment, we are nothing of value to others. In fact, isn't commitment a true sign of devout love? I think developing commitment is nothing short of being a great role model as a mother or father to your children and being committed to providing for their lives.

Commitment is like our baseline in determining and uncovering who we really are and how faithful we remain in all things. In my marriage, there was not equal balance and sacrifice; therefore, commitment was never grounded in true promise. It was about supply and demand. As long as I was giving what was expected in the relationship, sometimes being rewarded having played the part, then the image of a loving marriage was presented. It eventually became more like an obligation to be together, almost like the perfect looking politician's marriage seen on television. I desired so greatly to make our marriage work and for it to be authentic. I hope for our uncharted future, more people will value loyalty and commitment as I still do.

Secrets are the slow death of a relationship, and your emotional fortitude can prevail. Reaching out to other Christians to pray for you and your marriage is a reasob God put mentors and spiritual leaders in our lives. He knew we could not do it alone. Even when it is obvious that your spouse is hiding their phones, putting impossible and unbreakable codes on their phones, sleeping with their phones, changing routines to leave earlier for work and staying late; God still knows what is going on minute by minute. It is not for us to judge. There will plenty of time for all that in their future. We need to live with the highest level of unapproachable goodness to still honor God regardless of our situation. Life is bigger than us. Nothing stays the same. Growing our faith to a different level of knowing God will prevail and protect us to the very end. He never forgets his commitment and enduring love for us.

This is a favorite verse that shows God's great commitment.

"Humble yourselves, therefore, under God's mighty hand, that he may lift you up in due time. Cast all your anxiety on him because he cares for you." 1 Peter 5: 6 -7 NIV

God never leaves us or forgets us!

A Heart's Betrayal Workbook

Chapter Two Exercises

Small group format: 45 minutes

1. What is your definition of commitment? Is it Positive or Negative based?

2. Who demonstrated positive commitment to you? Parents, Teachers, other family?

   2a. If it is Christ, how have you demonstrated your commitment back?

3. How much is commitment is based on your culture? Discuss.

   (Group Exercise). Watch the movie "Joy luck Club 1993."

4. What has been your longest commitment in life?

5. Do you practice obedience in your marriage? How?

6. What are your boundaries that you are not willing to compromise in your relational commitment?

7. Are you honest with your spouse? Have you engaged in extra marital relationships?

8. How is conflict handled in your committed relationship? Do you know *The Gottman Method of the Four Horseman?*

9. Do you personally understand that true commitment is authentic loving when you do not feel like it?

10. How does Jesus show us commitment? How does he define love?

11. Commitment takes two very forgiving and invested partners. How often do you go for a check-up for marriage counseling?

12. Is your partner controlling? Does this honor God in any way?

13. Are you impulsive or self-centered? In what ways?

14. Are you willing to get counseling? Are you willing to humble yourself for change?

15. How does Jesus try to train us in goodness?

"The grace of God has appeared . . . training us" — not just "to renounce ungodliness and worldly passions," but "to live self-controlled, upright, and godly lives in the present age" Titus 2:11–12.

16. What does this above verse mean?

17. Are you willing to ask for help in your spiritual walk when needed? Who will you ask?

18. What is God's commitment to us? And do you know how to balance your commitment with light, hope, and redemption?

Chapter Three

How Do Others Harm Us: Domestication, Censorship, Co-Dependency and Narcissism

There are many ways to get knocked down and pushed around in relationships. For the intent of this chapter, we will focus on relationships that are filled with the unhealthy act of domesticating, censorship, and narcissist control with our partner. The push and pull of power in most relationships is normal. This odd desire for control begins at a very early age for us. Just like animals set hierarchy, humans fight for their place in this world. As little boys learn in school who is the leader in the classroom, little girls are also being subjected to watching the power struggle among their classmates. Later in life, this presence of power and unhealthy competition can be used to keep one person down and submissive, hence, the cycle of abuse begins. The initial stage of being controlled is allowing and submitting to acceptance. This state of being comes with confusion and disbelief. Subsequently, the person begins to feel embarrassment and has great shame of wanting to stay in a relationship that is dysfunctional. This keeps the cycle moving and the partner isolating more for the abuse to remain a secret while the protection of the abuser grows.

I have found that there are three main types of emotional abuse in relationships. Have you ever heard the word "domesticate" used as an adjective to describe ownership in a relationship? Maybe not, but you have generally understood the word used when talking about animals. Animals are either wild and feral or live indoors as domesticated pets. As pets gain trust in their owner, they become more reliant, losing some of their independence and natural instinct. I propose that a similar process occurs when some marriages and relationships become severely unbalanced. As one loses leverage and respect for themselves, the other partner gains control and dominance. Thus, one partner holds power over the other through taking more control in the management of the marriage; this can make the other partner feel helpless and dependent in some regards. Therefore, the process of domestication, enables one partner to live in an inescapable vortex. Eventually, some people get to a point in their relationship where they feel they are unable to do life without the other person making most of the decisions. This is obviously not a healthy union in a relationship and can eventually lead to resentment between the spouses. In some ways, domestication is a type of co-dependence and helplessness where the person feels they must be reliant on the other person to survive. I still can hear the whispers of my negative inner voice sometimes saying, "Should you leave?" "Is this true love or a marriage of convenience?" "Are you staying because of the low self-esteem you have been reduced too?" We must not allow our thinking to get the best of us. Tell yourself that these thoughts do not belong to me. Leave posted notes in your home to remind you that you are special, have a purpose, and are worthy of authentic Godly love and care in your marriage.

Not all situations of dependence are harmful. It can be necessary among those in a marriage where a person may be married to a disabled spouse who needs additional assistance in life, and this is part of making a lifetime commitment to another person. It is hard to know what a marriage may encounter over the years. As marital partners age, there is no guarantee they both will stay healthy. Some accidents happen throughout life that are unpredictable, and one partner may need the other to make all or most of the decisions in life for the good of the marriage. There is also the subject of some religious cultures requiring the man to take over most decision making. Keeping the various traditions and cultures in marriages can be a sign of obedience and part of being domesticated.

Censorship is another type of emotional abuse. One person in the relationship generally makes all of the decisions similar to above. The pure act of submission on the others part is a great example of how this works. Censorship can be cult-like. The imposing one-sided views based on their morals. This can cause the other person in the relationship to not be permitted to explore their own views, but instead, be a carbon copy of their partner. It is similar to mind programing. Have you ever heard of a family or couple who seems like a member of a strange cult? This is where everyone has to believe in a very similar way, or they are outcast. I experienced this for more than a third of my life. I had always been praised in my family for my inherent desire for independence. I believe that I was slowly summoned to believe in a religion that served no one except the legalistic viewpoint of the majority. It was terrible needing to go along with the herd and not allowing room for individuality or being able to think on your own and still be accepted and loved.

The cycle of abuse comes from many directions in a dysfunctional relationship. It is confusing to most sideliners why someone would stay in an insidious relationship of this nature. Nevertheless, there are so many reasons that people stay. One reason the partner stays is a lack of identity and fear of independence. This generally stems from a traumatic childhood. Marriage equals escape in some people's minds. They feel a sense of safety during the honeymoon period of dating. Hence, the person feels a sense of belonging and a false sense of freedom. They feel connected and the initial positive experience leads a person to believe they are loved and "at home." Leaving the relationship becomes difficult and impossible for some. The person is in constant turmoil and as mentioned before, their bucket of water is overflowing. To leave dysfunction we must acquest. Then we experience rejection and feel shunned if we leave. Self-doubt begins to enter and takeover. The fear can be unsurmountable.

There are countless types of psychological issues that many of us face. I consider the worst form of abuse coming in a form of control that is extremely damaging called narcissism. Narcissists and power-driven individuals are commonly excellent at this though it is achieved at another's expense. They tend to thrive on others' success only when it is tethered back to their well-being. Many believe this personality disorder most likely cannot be reckoned with or healed. Narcissists generally always want to be in control and desire the limelight to focus on the appearance of perfection and a charming demeanor. Not many people ever get close enough to narcissists, due to their secretive behavior flying under the radar. This type of destruction can take a toll on some women, especially mothers, which can promote negative coping skills such as self-harming and suicidal behaviors. The rise in depressive women is astounding. Anyone can google and research the correlation between women, mental illness, and abusive relationships with narcissists. Even though narcissists rarely seek mental health assistance, it is a genuine mental illness listed in *The Diagnostic and Statistical Manual of Mental Disorders, 5th Edition*, (DSM5). I must add to this area of thought that in the DSM5, Post Traumatic Stress Syndrome (PTSD) never really is seen or explained for its moral injury that can cripple us. I have seen and felt that crippling effect in my mind. The injury is sometimes hard to quantify and understand if one has never experienced the diagnosis. There is a book a highly recommend on this topic by Dr. Mark Alan Robertson, EDD. He was an emergency room chaplain that assisted first responders and combat veterans.

My memories of PTSD began when I thought I was going to be homeless while going through my divorce. I was hospitalized shortly after my divorce at Emory. That one night in the trauma unit was over $20,000. I did not have health insurance coverage which made me realize that mothers cannot always handle the stress and anxiety during and after marriages fail and lives can end poorly. My blood pressure was so high that I could have died. I am grateful that my doctor rushed me to the emergency room, and it taught me first-hand how serious our health can decline instantly due to a damaged and abused psyche. This is probably the reason I have great compassion for other women in similar circumstances and assist them in my position as a therapist.

Leaving a relationship that has great power over you is never easy. Often it is most difficult because of children involved. Narcissists generally come from a place of entitlement and great pridefulness. They will do anything to outsmart you and alienate your children. They may have been spoiled and indulged as an only child or as perfect piece to an already dysfunctional family. They also can be raised and indulged by narcissistic parent(s). I was raised in a middle- class family. I worked hard since the age of 15 and never knew what entitlement meant. After my marriage had crumbled as much as possible, I found myself having to support myself working three jobs while trying to maintain a somewhat normal lifestyle, having enough food to get through the week while me ex-husband living in the house. Money did not come in as the courts had ordered and it was unspeakable the conversations I had with my attorney and begging for just lunch money to get through my week. A narcissist will love to watch you squirm. You may often see them out of the corner of your eye smirking at you with a subtle laugh. It is the coldest and eerie feeling ever, especially when no one else is privy to see it. To know goodness, I think is to also recognize evil. The latter part of my divorce was the closest to encountering demons that I ever felt.

Many times, narcissists have endless resources, they are smart and wealthy, but will play the victim during the breakup or a divorce. They will make others view you as the weaker partner or parent. Their ability to command the love, be recognized in the spotlight, gives them endless attention, which they thrive on. While all that was going on, I was exhausted trying to avoid having attorney bills through the roof, and at the same time needed to put daily calls into the attorney so that the lights did not get turned off. One of my jobs during my divorce was in the emergency room, where I was a trauma assessment specialist. My shift was sometimes being called out in the middle of the night. It is heartbreaking to see all the women and men that had attempted suicide due to the brokenness of a love relationship, lack of support, and years of being controlled by another individual. I see nothing wrong with two people willing to conform. I believe it is very important in knowing what you're conforming to, who with, and how it benefits you. This can be difficult when you are manipulated.

I heard an amazing church sermon one day that I really loved about the Parable of the Good Samaritan. Jesus told the story in Luke 10:25-29.

The moral of the story is that there will always be some bad people but there are also many good people, good Samaritans. God always tells us to love our enemies. Hard to love enemies after divorce, but it's easier to allow healing and move forward. The Good Samaritan is a blessing – you will get a blessing.

The following questions will guide you through a better understanding to recognize false love, love bombing, deliberate manipulation, ghosting, narcissism, and how to escape a dysfunctional relationship with your sanity and integrity still in tack.

Chapter Three Exercises

Small group format: 45 minutes

1. There are many different ways that a controlling partner can hurt us. A person once healthy can enter into unhealthy relationship at any time. It can seem like an underground experience that many do not understand. This is why abusive relationships are often secret for long periods of time.

    Consider these possible issues:

    - *Learned powerless due to the trauma*
    - *Belief that they cannot make decisions*
    - *Hyper- vigilant Perfection*
    - *Sexual Dysfunctions*
    - *Mental Health Disorders*
    - *Physical Health Disorders*
    - *Loss of friends and neighbor*

2. How might you escape from an unhealthy relationship and the get help to stay away?

3. Are you being controlled against your will? Why?

4. While others may judge your relationship, they may also be trying to help you escape. Is anyone that you know trying to help you see another perspective of your relationship?

5. Do you have a history of unwanted and unhealthy relationships? What attracts you to others? Familiarity can be dangerous.

6. From 1-5 how is your Self Esteem? What part needs assistance?

7. How would you define your level of Self - Confidence? Please list 5 ways and explain.

8. Can you lean in on God and the Holy Spirit for direction and purpose?

9. What is your vision for a healthy relationship? What does it look like?

10. Make a list of 10 things you want in a lifetime partner. Highlight the things that are not negotiable.

    1.

    2.

    3.

    4.

    5.

    6.

    7.

    8.

    9.

    10.

11. Do you know how to determine if you are in a relationship that is abusive or with a narcissist?

Chapter Four

How Do We Escape Dysfunctional Relationships and Health Issues?

Sometimes we are not following God and his divine plan for us, therefore, we can become entangled in destructive relationships that God never intended for us. We decide that we know best and that we are in total control. SURPRISE – SURPRISE!

A best practice of getting to really know someone that we are dating can decrease your odds of living in a dysfunctional relationship. How often do we notice an attractive or a well-dressed person and want to get to know them? Maybe they carry themselves well in public or on the jobsite and we begin to admire that. What if you have just heard them as a speaker discuss a topic that you are passionate about and feel drawn to them. Even better, what if you are using an online dating app and feel an attraction to some of the words written or the photos in their profile.

I have heard many times a person saying that they love a movie or a sport game. Just because we experience something that aligns with our ideas of fun or attractiveness does not necessarily mean love. A person can dress like a sweet lamb and is nothing of the sort under the clothing. I believe that the importance and educational knowledge of human behavior can assist us through these trying times. I hear from my clients all too often how lonely they are and willing to comprise for love of another human being.

We all see and feel things differently, therefore, having various attachment styles. Due to our past, and different experiences in life some of us are healthy from the beginning while looking for a perfect mate, while others of us are dysfunctional in the area of love and continue the pattern. I think we have some insight or predetermined ideas of what we want. There are some excellent books that one can read on seeking healthy relationships and the questions in this chapter's study section can shed some wisdom when getting to know a new person.

There is basic sign of good character and the opposing person not possessing good morals and values. One example is when we are not equally yoked in relationships then trouble eventually surfaces. Your peripheral view will not be enough in this life, and you will not see certain things coming, however, age and varying negative experiences can be enough to detour from unhealthy relationships. Many things can be damaging to our sense of identity through the presence of someone else. The best advice is recognizing an outlier from the start. It may start as subtle oddities and then become very obvious. I always thought my intuitiveness would help me see through toxic relationships and now I know that is not true and anyone can be fooled. The decomposition of self is gradual. It is not always easily noticed until massive damage has occurred.

Dysfunctional relationships can eventually lead to a path of a variety of mental illnesses. The consistent pressure and strain can lead the mind to no longer function at its best. We become weakened such as an immune deficiency. Depression and anxiety start to creep in, and our strengths diminish. Sleep deprivation can be the beginning of the decline in both our physical and mental health disorders. Coupled with insomnia, poor eating habits and lack of exercise can lead to depression, anxiety, eating and sleeping disorders. These are just a few of the common conditions which can lead to more serious decline.

During high conflict relational indifferences, post-traumatic stress disorder (PTSD) and Disrupted identity, are conditions that can happen when a person experiences sudden or prolonged major changes in their life such as extenuated fear, and heighten levels of helplessness, constant shaming, continued stressors. Some of these may include break-ups, separation's, loss of job, and divorces. The DSM-5 states, "A markedly and persistently unstable self-image or sense of self." A key symptom is called Borderline Personality Disorder (BPD).

Major depression can occur after a major life changing event. A good example of this would be an individual who is unable to go to work, get out of bed, see friends, and eventually unable to leave their home. The DMS-5 states, Major Depression Disorder (MMD) "A common but serious mood disorder that is characterized by a low mood and negative emotions that last for most of the day. Individual and group therapy can be a wise choice in getting back to your "normal."

General to higher levels of anxiety can become unmanageable when trying to navigate unforeseen territory of loss in a relationship, thus, causing what the DSM-5 calls General Anxiety Disorder (GAD). This can be frustrating because all of the sudden your world is seen differently and no longer easy to live in nor navigate. My clients often describe it as a fog without any clearing, or a racing heart that never stops. Sometimes medication is a prudent option to get relief either long or short term. Therapy is another necessity to get sound support.

When your health has suffered enough, departing the toxic relationship to save your own mind, is when divorce becomes imminent. The Bible is clear that God hates divorce. I do not believe God likes any type of abuse from one person to another. Afterall, he made us to be partners and helpers in life. He gave us the beauty to be intimate, procreate, and have families. The idea of tearing one down or hatred was not the plan. God is our mentor and how did we get so far away from his love.

I think we are more likely to stay in a dysfunctional relationship based on what we have seen and practice in our own lives. I know I stayed in my very sick marriage too long. I kept thinking that my parents made it with their share of arguing and why could I not do the same. I used to believe that my marriage had a protection over it. I think things may have been different with good pre-martial counseling. We went once. There were warning signs that were ignored. The excitement of being a wife outweighed my better judgment. With proper Godly mentoring we might have made it or least not ended with such immense grief. God is a just God and did not intend for us to abuse one another in a sacred marriage or in any unequal relationships. They can end in bitterness, sickness, and jealousy destroying a piece of yourself.

If we choose "not" to end the dysfunction in the relationship, we can go to the Bible and read Nehemiah. He had lost his way. He had an internal longing and could not see his vision. Three things: Possibility, Problem, and the Passion. These things fueled him to rebuild the wall. He did not allow the distractions to tear down and snuff out his dreams. He had common distractions that we have today. His friends invited him to meet with them. He denied because he was focused, and intentions were to continue his great works. Then the people tried to extort Nehemiah, but he let them know there were only lying and trying to discourage him from his focus. Then the people bribed a prophet so that he would bring Nehemiah to the temple to be attacked. This did not happen. Have you ever felt like no matter how hard you try to focus that something gets in the way like a fog?

A heavy haze can come anytime in life and slow you down and you cannot see very far down your path. This is similar to life as distractions get in our way as well. We must know our problem well so our intentions can be strong and can be accomplished. So many distractions come in so many forms - friends, enemies, errands, and more. Try to live your life undistracted! If you are having intrusive thoughts telling you that you are worthless or your life in meaningless, be proactive and tell yourself that you refuse to own these lies. I believe there is a trap that our minds play. The only person that can stop it is you. Unfortunately, you may have been "groomed" to believe that the only person that can heal you is your spouse, the same one that has hurt you. In order to have holistic healing, which comes from within, is to let the person go that hurts you. Stop the chaos in your mind. They cannot rebuild you. Chapter nine and ten will further explain this.

What does fear do to the human race? It threatens us and can paralyze our lives as skewed thinking. Fear can manifest in our lives in many different ways. Sometimes fear leads to high anxiety, lack of motivation, but most of all, being blinded from seeing our full potential. If we are living a purpose-filled life, then the emotion of fear can be reduced. Fear resides in indecisive thinking. If I could have seen a little farther down the road in my relationship, then I would have known that the fog would lift.

Often, I felt like I was drowning with no life jacket in sight. This enhanced the feeling of being blinded by hurt and endless disappointment. Things do not always go as we hoped they would. But God has a good plan and a fulfilling purpose for you in life. Therefore, your purpose is walking closer to God leading your direction without question so you can see your path is clear.

Remember the story of the Greek Gods and the father that made wings of wax for his son Icarus. He told him never to fly to close to the sun. Icarus, leaving a life of captivity decided to live reckless and became very arrogant. Thus, let his guard down and was led by temptation to do exactly what he was warned not to do. Later, after being too close to the sun, lost his discernment and fell to his death. I believe we too can lose sight of the bigger picture in life and be held similarly in captivity while participating in dysfunctional relationships. We gradually fly too close to the sun and lose ourselves.

Do you want to be a survivor or surrenderer? You can know that God is there every step of your life and will assist you to power out of a poorly matched relationship. Knowledge and understanding of right and wrong, good and evil, and great compatible and happy relationships versus dysfunctional and mean-spirited toxic ones. There is so much support that you may not know about. There are hundreds of free support groups, shelters, specialized therapists, and that is the tip of the iceberg. Never give up. You may just need to ask for help to the right person.

A Heart's Betrayal Workbook

Chapter Four Exercises

Small group format: 50 minutes

1. Define dysfunctional relationship?

2. Are you in a dysfunctional relationship? If you are denying it, is this really truth?

3. What are some of the tale-tell signs of dysfunction in your life?

4. Is your self-esteem low? Is your mental health poor? How do you know? List 5 reason.

5. What needs improving in your awareness?

6. Why are you not important enough to stop the abuse? Are you flying to close to the sun like Icarus?

7. Are there reasons you may think you deserve abuse? Is it skewed thinking?

8. Are you ready to get help? Will you trust others trying to help and support you? Can you let your guard down?

9. Is there guilt or fear preventing you from starting fresh? What does living authentically look like?

10. Are you able to admit that you are living in a world of brokenness, addiction, and infidelity?

11. Who can help you rebuild? List names and things you can do to begin the process.

12. Will you consider really getting to know someone? Ask the hard and deep questions.

   a. Ask good questions. Open ended – What was that like? How would you describe that?

   b. Notice a person tone, energy and positivity. What makes you passionate about something?

   c. Do you feel safe and heard with them? Can you see humility and empathy in them?

13. Are you living a purpose-filled life? How are you able to see God's divine direction in your life?

Below please complete the exercise:

Use the hand sketch to illustrate by words or pictures all your strengths on one side and all your weaknesses on the other. In each palm draw what your strengths can do for you and the other side, how your weaknesses can be improved. If needed, add Alcohol Anonymous, Narcotic Anonymous, Emotional Anonymous, SMART Recovery, and Celebrate Recovery.

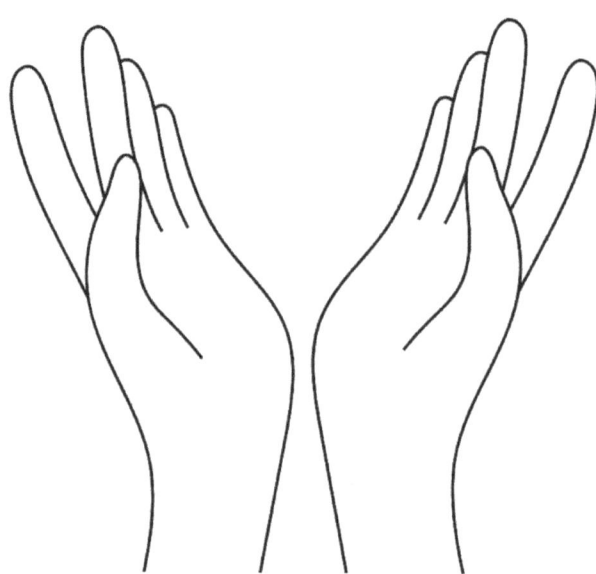

A Heart's Betrayal Workbook

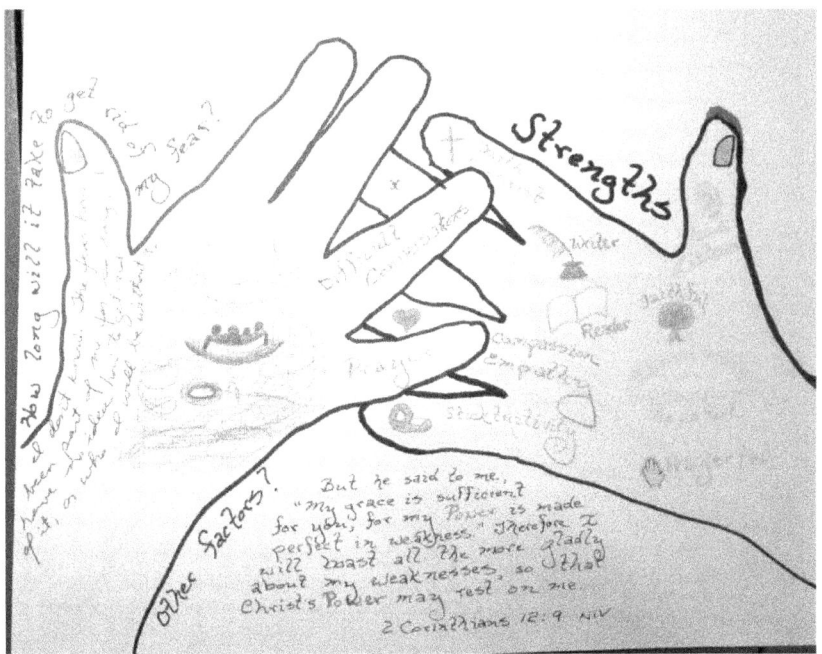

Above is a client's representation of her strengths, weaknesses, and growth in her life. She experienced two divorces that were abusive and is brave and courageous in sharing her life knowledge for the benefit of this book. This example can give you a brighter perspective on how the deepest of trauma experiences can be overcome and healing can be achieved.

Thank You, my dear, Trisa Marie Chancey.

Chapter Five

Effects on Our Children (Depression, Anxiety, PTSD) from Divorce and Broken Relationships?

I imagine that most authentic and compassionate parents love their children, but many children still do not feel loved during and after their parents' divorce. When children do not feel loved the repercussions are endless. Some dysfunctional behavioral signs include decline grades and do poor social skills in school, they have resistance responding well to too discipline, and can be filled with rage or anger. These reactions stem from the child having feelings that their brain cannot keep up with. Their emotional love tank is sinking while their internal attachment style is being formed. When the tank is full—meaning the child feels loved and safe by their parents—the child is predicted to grow up emotionally healthy. But when the love tank is empty, the child will grow up with many internal struggles such an avoidant attachment. Trust me, we never want their attachment style to deviate from a normal and secure style, the struggles are horrendous. Loving children effectively requires parents to express love in a language the child understands and often sacrifice things for themselves. Arguments and anger stemming for divorce should be handled by the parents behind closed doors. If we are wise parents, our children do not have to suffer from our parental poor choices.

A client recently shared with me that she never felt loved by her mother growing up. After her mother passed, this woman learned about the five love languages. She took the quiz online and then reflected on the fact that her divorced mother was always busy. Washing the dishes, cleaning the house, working two jobs and it was increasingly difficult (due to new financial circumstances) to spend quality time with her children. These are just a few ways divorce breaks the family unit. Children learn different viewpoints about marriage and relationships than we may choose. Often those children who feel unloved and fearful lose the balance of self-esteem and self-confidence.

Children often struggle with new stepparents. They do not want their parents to love someone else that is not their family. Children can have strong emotions over feelings of betrayal with stepparents moving in and taking over. They often feel alienated in their new surroundings. Alienation often begins to happen with one of their biological parents unless forgiveness and proper boundaries are set. Boundaries can also seem foggy for a child or teen who never receives proper restoration with both parents. They can bring these problems into adulthood with them and begin to have mental health issues. I see many clients that are still suffering from the past. They grow up as an unhealthy adult and can become resentful or the opposite a people pleaser." This people pleasing syndrome relates to being worried too much about a parent as a child. The child grows up thinking they must take care of others in order to feel normal. I will discuss more about the effects of the various attachment styles lead to issues within the children of divorce.

The understanding the negative effects on our children are practically inescapable. Divorce can be highly destructive and damaging especially in high conflict environments. Even the best of all parents cannot always shield themselves for the toxic circumstances of a mismanaged divorce. Most of us love of children and would go to great lengths to protect them. Truth is that sometimes this will not be possible. Even without divorce unfolding it is hard to always do the right thing for our children. A child generally looks up to the stronger parent. If it happens to be a boy, he often will look to his father. If the father is powerful and exhibits hatred his former wife, then what is a logical conclusion that how the son will grow up and feel towards his mother. Instead of a father trying to be his sons best friend during and after divorce he can be a strong leader and prevent alienation of a child and their mother by encouraging them to be obedient, loving, and respectful of their mother. Betrayal is a very powerful action and emotion. I have countless children that I have seen for more than 10 years that hate, despise, and are not willing to reconcile with one of their parents. It tends to always be the seemingly weaker parent who generally is the mother. This is all too often reflecting the injustice in our court systems and the imbalance of finances between two parents. There is more damage in our children's minds due to the unfortunate psychological warfare when pitting our children against the other parent when trying to present which parent has the most power, resources, and able to care the child(ren) best. That has to be the most pitiful way to measure caring for a child. Is it love and nurturing? Often this is so hard to see validated in court.

John Bowlby, a British psychologist, was extremely interested in attachment styles of children both healthy and unhealthy. He was the first person to come up with the attachment theory. He believed that many children develop an unhealthy attachment to others when they experience a high conflict and dysfunction divorce. They may struggle with various emotions, including anger, sadness, guilt, and fear. Frequently, children have difficulty adjusting to their new family situation and regiment. As a result, they often experience problems in school, friendships, or with their parents. A child who grows up with an insecure attachment style, has less security and trust in this world. They can be destined to living in an unhealthy relationship discussed in chapter 4.

Divorce can additionally have a greater negative impact on adult children still living in the home. They may struggle with feelings of loss and grief over the end of their parents' marriage. Moreover, experiencing changes in their future plans and spiritual journey. These changes can lead to increased stress, anxiety, hostility and anger, and heightened mental health issues.

Spiritual changes leading to religious abuse is common in power struggle divorces. Since there are four basic areas (Education, Religion, Extra Curriculum, and Medical) that are generally split and taken upon the parents this can lead to bias just for a parental win against the other parent. Parents have been the authority figure in the marriage can be seen as the leader of decision making. This can engage in spiritual damage through coercion within the faith of a child. I have personally seen many children in my years of therapy explain to me how they used to believe in God and Jesus and after the divorce, they find it difficult to still have faith. Generally, one of the parents lacks the interest to continue with church and other spiritual filling activities for the child. Keeping the motivation and commitment going when there is not a team effort, especially for teens will snuff out faith quickly.

Additional travesty's can begin when a parent engages in weaponizing scripture or sacred text for their own benefit. One evening I remember hearing the comparison that Jesus drank wine with his friends, therefore it is okay to drive to an undisclosed place and have drinks late at night with friends if they are from church. The Bible can say anything that you want it to by taking scripture out of context and giving it just the right twist in the presence of young ears. This brings me to a warning I once read.

"Any abuse or trauma done in the name of religion or deity associated with that religion can cause harm." (Matthew and Snow, 2017)

After a child hears overwhelming information that does not align with their faith or formal training, mass confusion can take place in the brain. The child or teen can begin to disassociate. This can be used as a coping skill to check out of reality. After doing this on a regular basis, the child can begin seeking unhealthy coping skills which leads us further and further from a safe environment for our beloved children. An identity crisis can transpire under severe duress. The child loses a sense of belonging to a mother and father unity. They feel like they must side with one parent or the other. The ideal of having Christians parents can be erased. Who and what they once believed is destroyed. A polarized view of Deity can be a serious dilemma. The following are just a few things that can develop - Difficulty trusting their own opinions, increasing maladaptive thoughts, balance issues fostering rational beliefs, distortion in image of God, and distortion establishing relationships in the future.

As I think back on my marriage it brings me to this conclusion. There is a leadership shortage in our nation of both men and women. We're not lacking people with big titles or authority. I think in many homes that as one of the parents rises to the level of ownership of a company or a sophisticated title within a company, family values begin to take a backseat. I believe that in a slow and subtle way there has become a lack of Christian mentoring and role modeling in many homes. Arlin Cuncic, MA, one of the magazine writers for, "Verywell Mind" states in her article about the people of entitlement; They tend to have sense of entitlement which stems from a personality trait. This belief is based upon someone thinking they deserve special treatment or recognition for something they didn't earn. People with this mindset believe that the world owes them without giving anything in return. (How to Spot a Sense of Entitlement in Someone that You Know. Arlin Cuncia, January 30, 2024). I believe that she is right! I see more and more of this in parents and then they pass this Andreus trait to their children leaving little room for the cycle to ever end. We all know that children of divorce are more likely to divorce as well. I hate that statistic and have always tried to instill in my child that marriage is for forever. There will always be some exceptions to the rule but to never focus on that. Marriage is sacred and not something we should want to get out of.

 I experienced the more a partner thinks they are important in life, they become a person with one excuse after another for less time spent in the home, in prayer, and family dinners or values. Wisdom and understanding of our children's needs is decreased as they watch the new changes unfold. Some will intentionally use the godliness in their lives to demonstrate or convince a fake or twisted biblical worldview. This type of leadership is not about character but of power. Instead, time and conversation are focused on their abilities, persuasion, and influence at work, in the home and often in the community. This infamous view they have can be so harmful it quickly destroys the ones that you once loved.

    The last topic of discussion is when one parent holds the purse strings (money) as a weapon over the other parent. Generally, the common syndrome of adult alienation sparks (AAS). Depending on the age of the child, much influence of money can lead to a false sense of love. I lived for many years after the divorce with that carrot over my head. I was unable to afford the glamours trips and big family dinners for many of the holidays and birthdays. The first six years after the divorce, I cried over losing my son to ski trips to Colorado that happen to be on most Christmas breaks and lavish vacation beach homes for summer holidays. It brought such destruction into the relationship. Truth is that many children are leveraged in the divorce in so many ways so that the weaker financial parent does not share equal time with their children nor has the same opportunities. These deliberate uses of power eventually will be seen and understood by your child. They all grow up and will have a mind of their own. That is my prayer for all children/ victims in families of toxic and narcissistic parents. I hold a certificate and many hours of training in reunification. It allows children without a voice or ones being heavily manipulated by the other parent, to try and unlearn the poison that has been forced for them to believe. It never gets easier going to court and fighting for these rights. It brings me peace to know that I am not put here to judge nor understand how one day each and every one of us and our despicable actions will be seen by God the Almighty. Turn your despair and worry into triumph. Being humble under pressure and pain is such a virtue. I love this verse to assist my mind towards growth and peace.

"Put on your new nature, created to be like God—truly righteous and holy." Ephesians 4:24 (NLT)

Chapter Five Exercises

Small group format

1. Do you understand parental alienation?

2. Did you suffer heartbreak from parental divorce or separation? Can you see the dysfunctional behaviors that need correcting in your life as a result of this behavior?

3. Do you know your Love/ Apology language? Please take this quiz in the Love Language website. What is yours?

4. Are you solid in your faith to stand tall and forgive what divorce has brought into your personal life in order to move to a healthier direction in the future? What does that look like?

5. Do you understand that some things in your personal divorce that happened to you may not be rectified in your timing? Examples Extra jobs, less time for children, alienation of children, chronic mental illness, physical illness, more stress and anxiety from individual parents.

6. Do you know your attachment style? Do you know your child's attachment style? Please take the quiz.
https://www.verywellmind.com/attachment-style-quiz-7562460

7. Do you need to make amends with your children? Is reconciliation possible? Are you praying daily for the union and reconnection with your child?

8. Are you part of the reason for alienation in your child's life?

9. Are you guilty of misusing your authority and persuasion in your leadership role as a parent that hurt your family? Is it time to tell your child what you have done?

10. Is it time to turn your despair and worry into triumph. Being humble under pressure and pain is such a virtue. I love this verse to assist my mind towards growth and peace.

"Put on your new nature, created to be like God— truly righteous and holy." Ephesians 4:24 (NLT)

Chapter Six

Legal Considerations and Extra Knowledge

From my vantage point, divorce was something I vowed never to allow in my family, and yet here I am. This proves that there are simply some things out of our control, or we waited too long to address, therefore, it became out of our control. When I was served my divorce papers, in an instant my ability to stay true to my beliefs and religion was challenged, not only by my husband but also from our legal system. I remember thinking, how can there be a law to dissolve my marriage when I made a commitment? Better yet, how can a legal system force my hand to sign away a marriage of 22 years. If I chose to ignore the papers and not sign them, there will be threatening legal consequences. It all seems so convoluted to me. My husband eventually made it easy for me to follow suit. There were many financial concerns that I could not overcome. If I did not sign the legal papers then my food and shelter would be cut off and the court would be left to tracking down my ex-husband to make things right again. It honestly is a game.

Many spouses do not understand that you do not have unlimited time to think about signing divorce papers unless you are wealthy or have an amazing kindhearted Christian spouse. I lost even more respect for my husband because he showed just how much he wanted me to loss everything by insisting to sell the family home quickly in the middle of January. My relator even told me he would call her and try to indicate that she was deliberately not trying hard enough to sell the house. This made her feel like he was accusing her of poor integrity. Common sense will tell that few families would buy a house in the middle of a school year and most homes do not sell in winter months in Atlanta. There were very few contracts under pressure to pick from, therefore, little time for negotiation and smaller profit to invest for my future.

This brings me to the next important topic of how to have the best mind going forward, so you do not agree to quick fixes under pressure and control.

Rule One

Stabilization. Mentally get a hold of yourself right away. It **IS** happening. You cannot wish it away. Be strong and check your emotions in the glove box. There is no place for it ... you must be ready to do business and in most cases your life will change for harder times ahead. I was 55 years old and that is not a favorable age and is professionally challenging to restart your life. As a therapist, I want you to express your feelings and get out the betrayal, just not with the court or attorneys.

Rule Two

Research and begin making appointments with expert and well-known attorneys for consultations. Do not delay. Every minute counts and the clock will wait for no one. If you have a partner who is preying on your last days of peace in your home, understand that your spouse can be vindictive and show little to no mercy. It can be your worst nightmare and literally unimaginable. I thought that I might not make it mentally or physically until my day in court. My attorney was going to request a protective order for me from the judge. I had pictures of over 10 unlocked guns in the home. There were a multitude of unsecured full liquor bottles also left in the house. Those two things do not make a woman with a young son feel safe or comfortable. I found it prudent to request an emergency hearing from the court but that is not an easy accomplishment with the family courts being so overwhelmed. It is so sad that I could no longer trust the man I married and spend a considerable amount of my life with to take these temptations for the marital home. Remember sins can be insatiable and drive out all morals, ethics, and faithfulness.

For this reason and so many more, you may need an attorney that specializes in victimization and spousal abuse. Again, it can be the hardest for women in their 50's and even older without an established well-paying career to have enough money for food and shelter awaiting a divorce. Be wise and diligent, it is your life. Start interviewing lawyers. I must have seen seven or eight. Be discerning and prayerful about each decision presented to you. Try to get a flat rate so that you may budget well. Many women find themselves bankrupt or their charge cards exceeding $30,000 before the process of divorce is even complete. Research well and complete as must leg work as possible to assist your attorney. Time is money. Understand your state laws about custody, alienation, and reunification. This is the worst of it. Do what is necessary to keep your sanity and wits about yourself. All things pass and there is another day to recompose. Do not wait on your former husband to show mercy or grace. This is a unicorn in today's society.

Rule Three

Go to all your financial accounts and other business alliances that you have shared while married. Do what is necessary for you to be able to understand your extent of wealth or debt. You cannot defend what you do not know. Take funds out if necessary and be honest with your attorney what is necessary to survive for six months to a year. This amount can be settled up closer towards the end of the divorce. You need cash flow to stay mentally coherent during this time. It will all catch up with you if you are greedy, sneaky, and dishonest. This is a very hard concept to embrace even when it may seem like an army of thieves are coming at you! It does not justify what is being done to you. Rise above others' behaviors. I received very little cash flow due to my part time job working in a mental hospital as a new therapist. I liquidated much of my 401K and my ex-husband insisted on the divorce to be rushed. Even a few months can seem like forever and mounds of debt when you are making under $2,000 a month. My ex-husband never paid any fees for my defense attorney nor the forensic accountant for what was his "requested divorce." This is a huge setback financially for most people. I kept remembering that God designed us and knows our needs. One of the most well-known promises of God can be found in the Book of Deuteronomy. Read it daily and gain strength from it.

"Be strong and courageous. Do not fear or be in dread of them, for it is the LORD your God who goes with you. He will not leave you or forsake you." NIV Deuteronomy 31:6

Rule Four

Do not get caught up in the dance of divorce. Sometimes divorce attorneys will use atypical inroads to intimidate you. This only instills more confusion and fear. You may feel vulnerable and that is normal. Just remember, you are not stupid. Play by the book and follow your attorney's lead with good integrity and merit. With good teamwork you will prevail and help you settle the case more productively and sensible. You are the co-pilot and have a responsibility in this situation. Your attorney is your mouthpiece and going forward into battle. Serious consequences can happen without responding wisely to what is happening. You may hate your situation and want to wish the divorce away but go forward with faith and peace. Do not lose your right to being present at all times because a verdict can be rendered without your presence. Hard to believe but very true. The law may seem like it rules and remember that God always has the last word.

After the divorce is final there are still facets of the divorce that leave us broken. Divorce is now a new entity in your life that could continue well into the future. There are many terms you will need to become familiar with such as arbitration, mediation, trial, co-parenting, alienation, and reunification therapy. Make certain to understand thoroughly. With children, divorce follows for many years. It was the worst part of my acceptance of being single. I just wanted all of the pain to end. Every day was a new discovery of more brokenness that one cannot conceptualize until it unfolds.

When divorce becomes a word on the table a person must consider how it will play out. For some people they can use arbitration. This is a form of alternative dispute resolution and can be a great and simpler choice when "uncontested." When both parties agree on most matters, they can tailor the arbitration process to their specific needs. This choice assists couples who are willing to not become unagreeable and instead have common ground during the division of items. This process allows individuals to avoid time-consuming, expensive, and burdensome court procedures. Not only may a divorcing couple arbitrate financial issues, but they can also resolve child custody issues (subject to court approval and oversight). This process of arbitration can work if both parties agree to agree.

For many others with vicious divorces, they may go to mediation where a seasoned attorney acts in the place of a judge. Their word is final and cannot be contested. It can be very costly and not end in an 8-hour day. In my case, a high asset divorce, I had to endure two days at 8-9 hours of mediation. It is meant to replace going to trial. You are still charged with paying your attorney representing you as well as the mediator. It can be mentally harsh and financially exhausting. Your outcome would probably still be financially less mediating than court. Sometimes you might negotiate with your attorney a set price. Mediation can be quicker and save precious time. Many family courts are so back logged that judges would prefer mediation to handle divorces.

There are many learning curves of what to expect in a divorce. While you need to be savvy and network, do not go too far where information becomes a blur. A divorce settlement is just a legal guideline. There is no such book that can be obtained for every rule of divorce due to the various state laws. Many states are more in favor of men than women. Note that there are still states that historically are conservative and still lean for mother's rights. There is always room for negotiation and compromise like bargaining chips. There are four basic areas without children. Separation, alimony, debts, and property division. When there are children involved it gets more complicated. These basics are added, for example, custody and visitation, child support, health insurance and health expenses for the children and, life insurance and future saving programs for the children.

What should matter in a settlement?

Do courts care about alleged or confirmed affairs? The answer is sometimes, if proof is evident and the mediator believes this can be considered a character flaw, more negotiation can be given to the other parent when considering terms of child custody. For example, more time can be allotted for a year then re-visited for the other parent to be given that time back. This means that the parenting plan can be contested and therefore, costing thousands more.

Here are some bits and pieces of extra helping information. During a divorce you may ask for any additional help in order to navigate the process easier. One perk that I investigated myself which turned out to be a little gold in the ruff was USAA. My ex-husband had been very brief in the military. He had benefits through USAA. I called one day to ask if I could have a charge card and future benefits. The answer was yes. Additionally, they offer transitional services for my move, nannying, and job placement. I later used them for loans and to rebuild my credit.

There is some good news in divorce. After many months, possibly years, it will all be just a bad memory that is hopefully replaced with fresh and healthy experiences. If I could have seen a little farther down the road and known that the fog would lift, I could have saved myself so much hurt and disappointment. We become somewhat blinded by our future during the divorce and forget our life is not over. Things do not always go as we hope they would. God has the best plan and is fulfilling purpose for you minute by minute.

A reminder, always be a good steward of your words. They are powerful. In just seconds they can bring a person to be inspired or empowered. Love requires kind words even when we do not want to. Be strong. Resist being mean and instead be a positive impact your person that you once loved.

Think about when we first learned words, it's sort of like little building blocks and for different ages we learn different intensities of words. As we become adult, we forget how these words were once built most like construction. Guard your mouth because it should build people and not tear people down even if someone is awful towards you. You do not have to react that way.

We can use words with great intent, and not for ourselves, but for others. This behavior will ultimately make people fall in love with who you are. Reference chapter one about who you are.

A Heart's Betrayal Workbook

*The Love of my love. Romeo and his bright servants heart.
May god always keep your safe and courageous.*

Chapter Six Exercises

Small group format: 50 minutes

1. Write down all the things you might need if you are served with divorce papers one day.

    -
    -
    -
    -
    -

2. Do you know where all the money, wills, and finances are located? A good wife is a wise one.

    Institution one:

    Institution two:

    Stocks and Bonds:

    Life Insurance Policy:

3. Do you know how to find a good attorney? (Super Lawyers) Do you know how many to consult with? Do you know what school they graduated, when, and if they have partners or paralegals to assist? Ask how many wins and loses they have incurred over the past year.

4. Do you understand the retainer and how it works? Hidden Fees?

5. Are you a good negotiator? Some divorces can be a flat rate.

6. Example of what to ask for in your settlement.

    a. Alimony – get an average of recent cases and overall state allowances

    b. Child and Custody Support – Detailed with all holidays included

    c. Property and debt – not always 50/50

    d. House ownership

    e. Insurance (House, Car, and Health) policies / Retirement funds

    b. Reimbursement for living expenses

    c. Reimbursement or mediation, attorney fees, and court fees

    d. Extended health and transitional services.

    e. Children's School Tuition, transportation, extra curriculum activates, school clothing, and books if in private school

    f. Jewelry – very tricky, beware: Diamonds, engagement rings and jewelry given as gifts. I did not realize my ex-husband could get a financial credit towards all of this.

    g. Counseling for yourself (One year suggested)

h. Training and education for yourself to have a lucrative career after the divorce

i. Reconciliation counseling for child and alienated parent

j. To use the tax credit for your child on your taxes

k. College fees until completed

l. Car expenses for your child

m. 501 set up with accountant / CPA and financial planner fees

7. Do courts care about marital affairs? What evidence do you need? Will this situation change the settlement? See if your state supports / favors the partners who is on the receiving end of an extra martial affair.

8. Can you try hard to see through the fog lifting when it is over? If not, what keeps you from believing it?

Chapter Seven

Mental Prison and Mental Health

If you are reading this book, you may have been robbed of living a life of independence and happiness through an array of hardships. I suspect that many readers have felt to be in a mental prison during and after a divorce or loss of a relationship. It is imperative that you put yourself first moving forward. No longer people-pleasing or burying and suppressing your pain. Do not fight it. Learn to sit in it and understand that it has a purpose. Think of waves at an ocean. Visualize you are bodysurfing, and the waves are high but will not drown you with a life jacket on. This example of turning on the safety mode behavior can be thought of as a cleansing. You may not see this immediately but as the journey unfolds it becomes more apparent.

This book opens with the very importance and understanding in our journey of knowing oneself. When an event happens and we are forever changed negatively, later we often seek comfort.

We can be cast aside with our sharp words quicker than unkind words in a marriage or serious relationship. The pain is immense and to get through tough things takes time. Do not give up on yourself and develop patience! God talks all about patience in the Bible. I love this verse. But if we hope for what we do not yet have, we wait for it patiently. Romans 8:25 (NIV)

I still remember one of the most significant events in my life other than my tenuous divorce. As I entered motherhood at 39 years old, I was forced to face the seriousness of life and death for my future child. The impact was unforgettable, time sensitive, and excruciating. Not only my health was seriously compromised, I was told in the beginning of my first trimester that my baby would most likely not make it full-term. Instantly, after receiving the sad news, I was surrounded by medical staff in a very large hospital's boardroom, to learn the devastating prognosis of the child and medical opinions from the hospital experts. I can still hear the echoing words and haunting suggestions of terminating my pregnancy by the doctors. I somehow held it together; I think maybe it was the feelings of numbness and then the intervention of my faith lifting me from the heaviness of the situation. My life as I knew it was no more. Hope and joy were stripped from me. I instantly felt my life was empty, filled with grief, and was spiraling down a dark tunnel. I was alone in my thoughts and the big rush of happiness of becoming a mother was extinguished in seconds. There were many gloomy days that I was very alone. My marriage began unraveling and who knew it would continue unraveling until my daunting divorce. I am still shocked that I never took one medication for anxiety or depression. I think it was a good choice at the time because later my husband during the divorce demanded all of my prescription records for court, trying to implicate, I was taking medications which made me less of a mother. I choose to lean into prayer and tried to balance my fears with the support of a small circle of Christian friends. God has protected me from mental health interruptions during my pregnancy and even to this day after my divorce.

According to the American Psychological Association, divorce can lead to increased anxiety, depression, and loneliness. It can also lead to decreased self-esteem and increased feelings of insecurity. This is particularly true for children who experience divorce. March 10, 2023

In my research, I found a very interesting concept. Psychology Today, Jeremy Clyman Psy.D. states; there is a condition named *divorce psychosis*. It's a form of insanity that emerges for a temporary period of time (the divorce itself) and remains within the ex-romantic relationship like an invisible toxic mist that distorts reality, blocks healthy impulses, and plays-up pre-existing character flaws. I believe that during, and for some time after divorce, many experience a loss of relative normalcy, making the dance of insanity spin at a high level. Some things are hard to accept and a spouse wanting to leave a once sought-out marriage can be hard to reconcile. As Christians, enduring pain in our lives can be a catalyst leading to better future. This is positive thinking and will help you make it through the process of high conflict.

In high conflict divorces, tragic allegations can be made that are completely true, or completely false, and somewhere in-between. Whether an act of spousal abuse actually happened, was subtly misperceived/exaggerated, or intentionally falsified, the point remains the same - two relatively normal people can mistreat each other so poorly, we can feel that we are losing our minds. This speaks to the sheer intensity of pain that divorcing partners cause each other. Once you have loved someone, emotionally committed, (developed expectations of a life-long story) and hitched your wagon to theirs (mortgage, children, etc.) that loved one betrays you by becoming rigidly unreasonable/overwhelmed (which, in turn, makes you rigidly unreasonable/overwhelmed), it's a long fall from grace to comprehend. Life starts to feel like a constant war zone when the home front creates stress instead of stability, and the "battle mode" perception that gets created out of self-protective necessity turns the other partner into an "enemy." Once you start perceiving/assuming/expecting an enemy...then an enemy, you shall get.

Your Mental prison can begin when you ignore this verse:

> "Therefore, since we are surrounded by such a huge crowd of witnesses to the life of faith, let us strip off every weight that slows us down, especially the sin that so easily trips us up. And let us run with endurance the race God has set before us. 2 We do this by keeping our eyes on Jesus, the champion who initiates and perfects our faith." Hebrews 12 1-2 NLT

Never give up perseverance, every day was an act of war during my divorce, it was so adversarial and miserable, even haunting at times. I felt my story came right out of a terrible Lifetime movie. I still remember hiding in the bedroom closet with my closest friend of thirty years. We were discovering and locating information for the trial that I was preparing for. All of the sudden we heard footsteps in the house coming our way. I thought my former husband had left for work, however, we both heard, his voice and somehow after leaving the home he knew we had entered the downstair bedroom. It was a time that I would never want to re-live and my friend never visited again.

I prayed daily for the dark entanglement of evil to be removed. Your mental prison ends when you realize that there is grace and forgiveness when you need it. There is always an invitation from God to be grateful and to forgive the past.

Below, this verse says it all.

"Let us therefore come boldly unto the throne of grace, that we may obtain mercy, and find grace to help in time of need." Hebrews 4 6 NIV

Most people going through a divorce will tell you that it's one of the most stressful times in their lives. Not only is your personal life in upheaval, but often your professional and social lives are as well. Finding ways to manage that stress is essential so you don't let it overwhelm you. Remember this classic nursery rhythm, "Humpy Dumpty sat on a wall. Humpty Dumpty had a great fall. All the king's horses and all the king's men could not put Humpty Dumpty back together again. My sweet neighbor and I spoke about this one evening. We concluded this is how we both felt over our divorce. It took a miracle – God to put us back together again.

There are several things to help manage the stress of a divorce. First, make sure to take care of yourself both physically and emotionally. Eat healthy foods, get plenty of exercise, and get enough sleep. Make time for yourself to relax and do things you enjoy. Seek medical help if need along with proper prescriptive care. Understand that biologically you can increase your input to lower depression and shame which are closely connected after trauma. The Cleveland Clinic 2022 states that the simple breakdown of neurotransmitters helps our body carry messages to the nerve and cell systems. These transmitters play many different roles in our bodies. Out of about an estimated 100 transmitters, the 4 basic transmitters which can induce happy feelings, regulate our moods, and balance sleep.

The first is Serotonin has one of the largest responsibilities on our mental health. Without enough of this we have disorders such as anxiety and depression, hence taking medication to replicate serotonin into our bodies. Dopamine, is another transmitter which allows us to feel pleasure and helps us focus. When dopamine is low, we can develop disorders and diseases as Parkinson's, schizophrenia, bipolar, attention deficit hyperactivity disorder (ADHD). There is a large category of medications to assist in these disorders. Endorphins are essential in life because they help with pain tolerance. This is not just physical pain but also mental pain like sadness. The endorphins help with balancing our moods. The last neurotransmitter is oxytocin. This natural hormone made by our brain assists many mothers in child labor and the lactation for their babies. Oxytocin is so amazing because as other neurotransmitters it also effects our human behavior. It helps with sexual arousal, trust, bonding, and relational attachment. It's vital role is essential in living a healthy life as a mother, father, girlfriend, boyfriend, or any other relationship that relies on trust and bonding. (https://my.clevelandclinic.org/health/articles/22513-neurotransmitters)

God weaved the perfect plan for our brain to be in sync with our bodies. When we lack the capability to rid ourselves of depression and shame naturally medication management is often required. The platform of reconciling and forgiving others and you is linked to the availability of some of these neurotransmitters. It begins to all make sense as soon as you are able to see the puzzle coming together. This is not always an easy task. The lower our natural production of serotonin, dopamine, endorphins, and oxytocin the less ability to manage our emotions.

When we are in an emotional upsetting and weakened relationship that has little tread to keep on the track, looking for relief can come in several areas. I traveled through many marriage counselors, some and good and some not so good. Some were extremely expensive and not so great, and others seemed to be innately gifted and worth every penny. As a Christian and seeking a faith-based counselor, I met many different personality types. Some made me felt safe and others, I wanted to run out the door at the first fleeing opportunity. Make certain you align with your counselor, and they have experienced similar feelings and experience to be more relatable. Ask for book, group, and medication referrals. In addition to therapy there are many natural remedies to help in times of despair and depression. Exercise, socialization, eating well, and proper sleep and hygiene. There is a great verse of asking God for assistance and him bringing you relief. Proverbs 16:9 NIV says, "In their hearts humans plan their course, but the LORD establish their steps."

Chapter Seven Exercises

Small Group Format: 30 minutes

1. What is a mental prison to you? Where is the key located to peace?

2. How do you function when you feel paralyzed? Who gives you strength? Favorite verse?

3. What is it like to have genuine grace? How do you know it is there?

4. Look up the following verse. What is Hebrews 1 12 trying to say to us?

5. How can we find grace when it does not seem possible? Who are our ethical and spiritual mentors?

6. Are you embarrassed to ask for help? Why?

7. What can be your favorite verse of strength?

8. Do you feel like Humpty Dumpty? How can you gain peace?

9. What are the basic 4 regulating neurotransmitters that help us in physically and mentally?

10. What does each do and how can you get more of these added to your daily blood system?

11. Medication is always a great choice when need to relieve stress, anxiety, and depression. What are some natural methods to increase balance and happiness?

Chapter Eight

Reconciling and Forgiving: A Healing Homecoming

The first commandment in the Bible alone "requires total dedication to the Lord throughout our whole life. The demands of this one commandment alone requires 100% commitment 100% of the time for 100% of our life." Therefore, reconciling your marriage is an excellent choice. I realize this cannot be done all of the time, but I suspect it can be done much more than we think.

Source: https://dailyverse.knowing-jesus.com/luke-10-27

Reconciling and forgiving ourselves is not an easy task. When we finally know that we are in a weakened relationship that has little tread to keep on the track, giving up can seem be a viable choice. Pray about the choice to reconcile or to move forward and depart with great forgiveness. This can lead you down a winding path of the unknown. You will need to know what is a true homecoming? I believe reconciling with others is the first step to accomplish this. It can still seem painful even after this step is completed. Forgiveness is when the pain begins to dissipate, and humbleness grows closer and connects to our God.

Reconciling can often begin in a counselor's office or at church. I traveled through many marriages counselor's during my journey in marriage. Many were expensive and not that great. Some were advertised as Christians and were confusing. Others were of different faith and had sound solutions. I believe that God provides gifts to his people with healing abilities. Your mind probably goes to a doctor's image when thinking of healing. However, good therapists have incredible healing gifts when guided through Christ. I have met many different personality types of therapists and felt safe with some and others I wanted to run out the door at the first fleeing opportunity. God's gifting to his people is plentiful and never give up praying about the right counselor to walk alongside your healing process.

I believe forgiving takes place when you genuinely are in touch with your heart. Your heart can be contaminated by a lack of love from past or present experiences. I feel pretty certain that your heart is the command center of your soul. There is a prudent verse that aligns with this statement. Proverbs 4:23 NIV, "Above all guard your heart for everything you do flows from it. Could this be any clearer? If you are confused about your inner core this is where you can find it. Many psychologists will talk about your inner self and internal dissonance. I remember in school I learned that this term internal dissonance is where conflict is created. Sometimes this is related to people who are avoidant, ignoring, or dismissive. Is this a part of your personality traits? If so, hold on because we have some work to done before getting to forgiveness. Did you know that dissonance causes us to overreact, and to mis-interrupt many situations. Barriers begin to rise and the next thing you know, your relationship is sinking like a tugboat! Personal relations do not need to be this difficult. Be conscious of your levels of empathy and treating the ones that you say that you love. Many of us could have lived in our marriage with hypocrisy and misapplication of what is good for our hearts. This causes mass confusion about our heart. In the Bible, Matthew chapter 15:11, there is a lot to learn about the truth of our heart. It is not so much what we put in our mouths but what comes out that defiles us.

    Has anyone ever taught you to monitor your heart? There are a few steps that I think will help you. First, beware of your language and the words that leave your mouth. The tongue is the sharpest weapon that you have. Words cripple sometimes and leave others paralyzed. Words can give life just as quick it can give death. Again, Matthew 15:19 NIV, clearly teaches us that from the heart comes evil thoughts, murder, adultery, sexual immorality, lying, and the verse continues. This causes personal impact with others that is not good. I lived through this, and it almost destroyed me. Is this something you want to be the maker of? Monitor whether or not you are storing good things or bad things in your heart. What is on the inside of your heart eventually comes out. Did you ever wonder if your integrity is as high as you believe it to be? I think that we are all like a piece of candy with a shell on the top. To simplify this idea, when we least expect it, someone penetrates out shell and something we may not expect comes out of our mouth. This is like a chain reaction and happens quickly. When we are not ready to be vulnerable, our heart may speak from a root of anger, shame, or even envy.

    Second, how often do you do dig below the surface? Is it time for a cleaning in your heart's storage shed? To monitor the heart's health status, it is probably time for a deep cleaning. I bet you will find a lot to clean up. Remember those hurtful words from your spouse? Even worse, your child that repeats what his dad may have said to hurt you and now it is repeated. Cleanse the dissonance in your heart so that only goodness came emulate. Do not give yourself an opportunity to overreact due to the dirt in your heart. Identify and replace those things that are lounged in negativity with goodness and purity. Get the splinter out or the thorn in your side. Your words can be irrational and need assistance. Be a leader and a role model worth following.

Third, allow your heart and mind to be renewed. Imagine you without passive aggressive behaviors, sarcasm, judgement of others, and replaced with the curiosity of other wounds, dreams, and hopes. Can you see what is true about your current self? Do you know who you really are? That is why it was so important for me to begin with chapter one of this book entitled, do you know who you are? Do not be the one that steals these things and is hurtful to other hearts.

In the Bible, the book of Luke, explains well our sinful nature and kindness of forgiving. The prodigal son was welcomed back in a homecoming of greatness. The great parable about the father and his sons is known even in circles of non - church people. It is about how we are all sinners. God is continuously forgiving us. Why is it so hard for us to forgive others? I often think our pride clouds our true vision. God never loses, not even one, of his flock. He has open arms for us to come home to at all times.

We all have our reasons why we feel some things are unforgivable. This is not biblical. One of my favorite verses is Luke 15:7 NIV.

"There will be more rejoicing in heaven, over one sinner who repents than over ninety-nine righteous persons who do not need to repent."

This can be a hard topic to swallow for those who feel they are obedient and in God's favor. Truth has it, that we all need rescuing and made whole again through God. We need to come back to our basic faith more often and be healed through the acceptance of forgiving 99 times x 99 is the narrow path for internal healing. Why have we become so judgmental and think we should be allowed to swing down the gravel? Our self-righteousness keeps us from forgiveness which keeps us from fully healing. Hatred keeps us from seeing clearly on this matter of forgiveness.

Another means to learn how to forgive. Take the added sections of the Love Language Quiz entitled, *Anger and Forgiveness*. These are the main things that you will learn and the intensity that it holds for you to move on with your life. Most of these are self-explanatory, nevertheless, take note of your style. For instance, if you always hoped that your ex - partner would come to you and accept responsibility for an affair but never did, can you move on? Of course. Is it easy, of course not, but you are able as a child of God to let it go. Without this step to acknowledge you may never move forward in a healthy manner.

- **Make Restitution**
- **Planned Change**
- **Request Forgiveness**
- **Expressing Regret**
- **Accept Responsibility**

Losing your judgmental beliefs for others can assist your walk in the spirit. Forgiveness is biblically required of all of us. When we are filled with the spirit and feel compassion for others (even if they have harmed us) it is better living. Sin breaks people and also breaks God's heart. You are in control of what you think and do. Make it a daily intention to be in sync with God and live in a direction of love. Below are things that can harm us in our walk and hold us back from goodness.

Religious Abuse

Parents have an authority figure status and can be seen as leaders. Therefore, can engage in spiritual damage through coercion to conform as legalistic. Instead, meet your children where they are. Do not judge and love like the father.

Many weaponize the scripture or sacred text. The Bible can say anything that you want it to by taking scripture out of context. Rule followers can often not see beyond the log in their eye. I have respect for the following quote.

Now the child or teen starts to disassociate. An identity crisis can happen, and the child loses a sense of belonging to a mother and father unity. They feel like they must side with one parent or the other. The ideal of having Christians parents can be erased.

Do you know what a Polarized View of Deity means?

It all begins with minimizing your opinions and accepting that you cannot possibly know it all. Shocking and correct. Many of us through our tragic moments in life have difficulty trusting which leads us to a lack of developing self-trust. We doubt ourselves constantly which presents many maladaptive thoughts. This is not a truthful or healthy way to live life. Instead, we need to ask God to assist us in fostering more rational beliefs. To give a clear vision of who God is instead of the distorted image of God that can run through our minds. We all need positive ways to view the best version of ourselves and to establish positive relationships in our future.

As C.S. Lewis once said,

"Humility is not thinking less of yourself but thinking of yourself less." This very thought process will lead us down the correct path of life.

Let me remind you, life is hard! It can seem impossible, but it really is not. Our state of mind puts us in places that our perception does not tolerate well. Vernon Howard stated:

"Never fear, deliberately, walking through dark places that is how we get to the other side of the light."

ns, LPC

Chapter Eight Exercises

Small Group Format: 30 minutes

1. How often have you forgiven someone this year?

2. How often do you forgive yourself? What does your method of forgiving look like?

3. What are those things keeping you from true forgiveness?

4. Say out loud, "As a Christian I need to be someone who learns to forgive freely again and again."

5. What steps do you need to engage in to cleanse your inner heart?

6. What are your favorite Bible verses that help you lose your pride or anything that may stand in your way of forgiveness?

7. What condition is your heart in? Where do you need to clean it up?

8. Do you believe what Vernon Howard stated?

9. What is the best version of yourself?

Chapter Nine

Singleness and Rediscovering Yourself

Have you thought about what might be like to be single again? It could be fun. It will take time to acclimate again and that is normal. It is hard going from the title or a wife to now a single woman. It is like when you were getting married, and your veil was pulled down upon your face. Then the veil was lifted, and you felt your first kiss as newly married bride. Now, you can lift the veil again and begin living a life as a newly single person. I know it is such a loss of losing your marriage and it also can be seen as a healthy gain.

Bowling Green University has reported that older American women generally remain single longer after divorce when compared to men. That does not mean having fun and dating is off the table. It may mean that independence is nice for a change. Remember that having a positive relationship with yourself is the most important thing for emotional stability. You are trying to find out who you are again. You are becoming more self-reliant and trusting again. Find your true north and passions again.

"If you are depressed, you are living in the past. If you are anxious, you are living in the future. If you are at peace, you are living in the present."

Lou Tzu; ancient Chinese philosopher, founder of Taoism

Mental fitness is the first step. Understand that your grief many be inescapable for a period of time. It is a choice when to decide to recover. Your darkest hour only had 60 minutes in it. You've got this! Do not fall back into the ditch you just spent hours digging yourself out of. Truth is that you can continue suffering in thoughts and dysfunctional memories or you can find the meaning and future hope to move on. A "Broken Heart Syndrome" is real and can be fatal. A breakup or other traumatic emotional stressor can be enough to cause physical damage to the heart. This can lead to a severe condition where the heart muscle has failure. It can bring you to the emergency room. I witnessed many cases. It imitates a heart attack and is referred to as takotsubo cardiomyopathy.

This was discovered in 1990 when the Japanese believed the condition was the weakening of the heart muscle. *Takotsubo* is the Japanese term for a kind of pot specially designed to catch octopuses. The syndrome brought about the examination the hearts of early patients suffering from this condition. The researchers saw the same type of appearance as the takotsubo bowl. The apex or tip of the heart balloons out during the attack and the base of the heart contracts normally. Then the muscles tighten up and the heart enlarges. It can be sharp and fierce pain. The good news is that broken heart syndrome is usually treatable. Around 1% of people with broken heart syndrome ultimately die of it, according to Cleveland Clinic 2023. While this seems low if you think about 1% of our population that is a big number for death.

An example of this is when the actress Debbie Reynolds, the mother of Carrie Fisher, died just hours after her daughter's death. It may also explain why couples who have been together for long periods of time die within months of one another. This does not have to be your experience!

(https://www.nbcnews.com/news/us-news/broken-heart-syndrome-are-symptoms-causes)

(https://health.clevelandclinic.org/can-die-broken-heart-emotional-questions/)

Building a new life after divorce is living your life in the present and is a large part of healing. Remember, you are not alone. There of hundreds of thousands of people experiencing the same or similar feelings as you all around the world. Have a plan to begin again. Push the restart button! Step One – Ask yourself:

- What kind of life do you want?
- What kind of lifestyle do you want to lead?
- What goals will this take? (More education, experience, mental and physical endurance)
- What is your creative outlet?
- Begin networking for new friendships and social outlets.

As stated in the prior chapter, forgiveness is a necessary part of the answer to healing from a spiritual standpoint. What do you need in a relationship and what type of partner will be best for you? Here is a thought. Make a list of some things that you are looking for in a new individual. Here is my top twenty-one.

1. A man after God's heart (prays with his wife and family).
2. A man of honor (goes without defining).
3. A man filled with valor (can be a mentor to others struggling in marriage).
4. A man of integrity (does not put himself in vulnerable situations).
5. A man of faithfulness (asks for help and accountability before being tempted to cheat.
6. A man of gratefulness (embraces the differences between a man and woman).
7. A financially responsible man and plans for the future for his family (does not ignore God's plan of responsibility).
8. A man of laughter (not at his wife but instead with her).
9. A man of great listening abilities (actually cares and)."and listens genuinely."
10. A man of vulnerability (honesty and morality).
11. A man without pride (putting his family first).
12. A humble man (not just in front of others but consistent and authentic).
13. A generous man (not just for their own benefits).
14. A man with a transparent and loving heart (without secrets and lies).
15. A man with a strong, compassionate heart (that doesn't leave while his wife is ill or traveling to explore other marriage breaking options).
16. A man of balanced sensitivity (who does not ignore when his partner is in pain).
17. A physically strong man (who is active, healthy, and doesn't sleep all day and mentally check out most weekends hours).

18. A man who thinks out of the box and enjoys resolving issues instead of hiding and ignoring them.
19. An exciting man who loves to do things together with his wife instead of always focused on business, and taking employees away to continuous trips and so-called team building events. This gets in the way of true Christian family time and the idea of wholeness and trust.
20. A man who delights in exploring and traveling together to see God's wonders.
21. A man that applauds a woman of independence and also loves her tenderness without exploitation.

Never forget the pain takes you to places you never thought were possible. It strengthens you and makes you able to continue your journey. We must choose to live and defeat any intrusive thoughts about being single or finding another relationship. Grief can spike at any time. It is more than a feeling; it is a place you go in your heart. You either choose to survive the pain or die with it. I remember when I was told by my son's doctors that he was going to likely not survive at birth. It felt like a cannonball ready to explode inside my gut, heart, and mind. I chose to think the positive and not allow my love to become interrupted or derailed. Things worked out for my son. In divorce, the loss is hard to conceptualize. The sadness is our conscious mind which continues to look for the person that we lost. When we accept that they are gone and the death of the relationship that once existed, then we can more on to a healthy mindset of singleness. Here are some easy steps:

1. Accept the reality – You will move forward.
2. Experience the pain – This may feel like a robot and very disconnected.

3. Adjust to the new environment and have gratitude for it., because no one knows it

It is good to know what type of grief is keeping you isolated and depressed, because no one knows it better than you!

5 years after my divorce just getting back to a normal life.

Normal Grief

Numbness, depression, reorganization – this is a must because you cannot stay here forever, recovery- there is a push and pull, recent believed depending on your culture 6 months to 2 years. Grief be a gift.

Anticipatory Grief

No date but understand it is coming. A feeling of dread and cannot figure out how to stop it.

Elderly parents, cancer, other illnesses, awaiting DIVORCE.

Disenfranchised grief

What if we did not have permission to grieve? Forbidden relationship, work wife, work colleague. A secret connection, interrupted love with little way to express. Story telling is the best healing.

Complicated Grief or Traumatic Grief

Prolonged and intense grief associated with substantial impaired. Feel foggy.

Accepted prolonging and pinning for the lost person

Problems accepting death

Not enough time or only depending on time alone to recover

More deaths than just one

Other mental health disorders

Bitterness of the loss

Example- we are in this now from COVID

DSM5 – Prolonged grief after 6 months F43.81

Another form of therapy that assists with our healing and reconciliation is called EMDR, Eye Movement Desensitization Response.

This specialized type of therapy helps work together client reality and reality in the present moment. Human pain and serious damage cause a disconnect in our brain and later numbs the ability to experience happiness and goodness. This is typical of clients with trauma due to tragedy and not having good coping skills.

Feelings Butterflies by Mary Natalie Chancey

A good frame of reference is during and after divorcing our brain can still begin rewiring depending on survival mode. Some of us will turn to drugs, alcohol, outrageous anger, and severe depression coupled with anxiety. Many women that I have treated explain the basic tents of survival seems gone. As these clients try to integrate a new life including loss of being a mom and a wife, some believe that lack of finances and love end up losing themselves by disassociating behaviors just to survive. This is very common in addiction. Our bodies are designed to cope with life. The physical mental piece the body numbs out a certain level of pain. The pain can surpass more than the body can handle then a gap opens, and addiction begins. Pure survival mode is very similar to a narcissistic. The rewiring is taking place. All the years of feeling undermined can end. The psychological piece of the pain of divorce can end. It can feel almost like detoxing an internal conflict that never ends.

You must really listen, understand what it is like to live in extreme pain, and know how to stabilize your inner thoughts. Remember you are not designed to be a turtle with your head inside your shell. Allow yourself the freedom to explore the idea of a new self. You have another opportunity of being happy with you! Who are you now? Try our new hobbies and see where you can shine. Date when you are ready and enjoy the courtship again. Most of us have an innate desire to be loved by another person. Maybe it is time to find a more suitable mate, get into therapy, and explore eye movement desensitization response (EMDR.)

Chapter Nine Exercises

Open Forum in large group format: 50 minutes

1. List coping skills that will work for you as an individual?

2. Write a personal prayer that you can memorize:

3. Is it okay with your soul that you are single?

4. What boundaries will your singleness have?

5. Have you tried Eye Movement Desensitization Response (EMDR) therapy? Why?

Below is a list of things to put in your back pocket and bring forward when needed.

- Give yourself daily affirmations of love, strength, and faithfulness.
- Daily prayer for motivation and continue in a forward direction.
- Double check your boundaries: Stay away from negative people or energy vampire that drain you.
- Practice learning new things and stay involved in things that matter to you. Community work, volunteering, renewal workshops, new friendships, join clubs and support systems, and add new hobbies to the mix.

- Learn to let your creativity flow and healing to begin.
- Stay social. Never give up. Isolation is dangerous. This life can provide good things still awaiting your discovery.

Below are ideas of how unlimited our world can be in new hobbies which can be a positive and creative way of mending minds:

1. Learn about Yoga. It can be a unique source of inner healing. When a person is able to be still, quiet, and in a vulnerable position, they can heal. The healing process can be sneaky. Why? I do know when I see tears flowing down a person's face, therapeutic healing has begun because the body feels and remembers past pain. This fact has been mentioned already in my book. I think this type of healing is awe-inspiring. Remember that the darkness can steal peace and uncomfortness. This can prevent and slow down the healing. Be mindful and have grace with yourself.
2. Learn to make a piece of art that resembles your pain in a restored version. Keep it as an example of your progress and successful, trending to the new version of yourself.
3. Write a book or memoir about your struggles and ways of healing to assist others on their journey.

Resources

- American Academy of Matrimonial Lawyers: https://aaml.org/
- DivorceNet: https://www.divorcenet.com/
- American Bar Association: https://www.americanbar.org/groups/family_law/resources/divorce/
- National Center for State Courts: http://www.ncsc.org/Topics/Family/Divorce-Custody.aspx

Applicable Law in the U.S.

- The Uniform Marriage and Divorce Act: https://www.law.cornell.edu/uniform/marriage_divorce.html
- Divorce Laws by State: https://www.lawyers.com/legal-info/family-law/divorce/divorce-laws-by-state.html

Works Cited Notes

1. Ingalls, Nick and Nelson, Kate. "Relationships - Marriage, Problem-Solving, and More." Verywellmind.com. Feb 2024.

About the Author

Christine Cantilena Barnes became a Christian when she started to understand the depth of brokenness in her life at an early age. She was able to recognize right and wrong from her training and practiced moral standing from her parents. She went to church weekly and was baptized as a child in her famiy's Catholic Church. Later, she made her first communion, and then her confirmation of faith. These were all the steps united with her family's faith. It was not until later in life that she began thinking that something was missing in her faith.

The past glimpses of brokenness throughout her childhood and college years drew her closer to God. Many years later, the pinnacle of her faith was tested and reached when her son was born in 2004. He was diagnosed with a deadly condition called congenital diaphragmatic hernia (CDH) in utero, a rare condition in babies that required several surgeries and constant care. In her late thirties, she believed this difficult journey helped her to see not only the fragility of humanity, but also the amazing connection that comes from extreme vulnerability and helplessness to allow God's will to be done. She is a devoted mother of one son and continues the battle for future mothers walking in the difficult paths of trauma, including high-conflict divorces and finding closure after a divorce.

Christine has worked as a licensed professional therapist (LPC) and as a certified professional counseling supervisor (CPCS) in several hospitals since 2014, serving the mental health public. She was a staff member at Peachford Hospital, Ridgeview Institute, and the various locations of Emory Hospitals. Her training focuses on trauma, difficult transitions, anxiety, prolonged grief, and resistant depression. Her goal is to serve those desiring healing and uncovering core reasons for negative patterns of self-harming behaviors, suicidal ideation, high anxiety, and specializing in persons facing divorce, child alienation, and relationship separation.

Christine holds a Bachelor of Fine Arts from Virginia Commonwealth University (VCU) and has a specialized art degree with skilled training in drawing, painting, and design that can be used for therapy. She owned horses and helped one of the first physical therapy groups in Richmond, Virginia, assisting children with walking disabilities through therapy on the horses. She holds a master's degree in clinical mental health counseling from Mercer University and specializes in dialectical behavior therapy (DBT), sand tray, and eye movement desensitization and reprocessing (EMDR). She holds an advanced academic certification from Virginia Commonwealth University (VCU) in Criminal Justice Administration while also trained in forensic evaluations for court and parental alienation. Most recently, she has been a guest on the radio show "Divorce Town" and assisted women in crisis.

Christine believes "There is a solution to all problems." Everyone in life has a story to tell. We all want to be loved and listened to. She embraces all eight of psychologists Eric Erikson's Life Stages and Abraham Maslow's Prominent Personality Theory. She hopes this book will educate others to form authentic relationships, see their blind spots, get closer to God, and heal from depression, anxiety, and complex post-traumatic stress disorder.

"Chase after the golden narrow gate, it will lead you to a better life with peace, joy, and authentic love. With proper self-care and extended self-control, a person can have real fulfillment and flourishing faith regardless of your past trauma. A survivor means you are alive. The best is still yet to come!"

Christine Cantilena Barnes

Also By
Christine Cantilena Barnes

www.ingramcontent.com/pod-product-compliance
Lightning Source LLC
Chambersburg PA
CBHW061748070526
44585CB00025B/2836